WHEN *life* MEETS LEADERSHIP

www.whenlifemeetsleadership.com

ISBN: 9781475087697

Printed by CreateSpace
Designed by bluespace creative, inc.

Dedication

Like happiness, life's gifts do not decrease by being shared.
Many contribute. Many enjoy. You are next.

Table of Contents

WHEN LIFE MEETS LEADERSHIP

Square One

The answers are deceptively simple.
It's the questions that you find while achieving them
that can take a lifetime.
-Authors of When Life Meets Leadership

Do you ever have those days or moments when you feel like you're "running on reserve battery?" You're thinking, "How do I handle this situation? I certainly didn't expect that reaction from him? Why am I being misunderstood? Does she really believe I would do that on purpose?"

Life hands us so many challenges and opportunities; it can be daunting to think through, plan or even react to different situations. How about a framework you can access with little effort and full confidence? A simple, compelling, balanced framework composed of four words that you internalize, develop, and have quick recall of to assess and act in any situation – as you live your life and lead in life.

How do we know it really works? Because among the four of us (the authors), we have more than 135 years of experience in multiple family configurations, business endeavors and leadership challenges. Every time we would share the power of The Framework composed of the four P's, someone would write back or stop one of us to say, "It works – here's what happened." These were everyday people from every walk of life. In fact, in the following pages you will find in-depth interviews of "everyday people" who exemplify PEOPLE, PURPOSE, PASSION and PERSEVERANCE.

We took to heart people's comments that we should write a book. "Why not?" we decided. Instead of just sharing The Framework with the groups we facilitated, classes we taught, or people we loved, we could share it with everyone. Our mantra became "Write it in a way that every person can understand, personalize, and actually implement the four P's in their lives – simple, compelling, balanced!"

As human beings our power initially comes through our minds, then travels to our hearts, triggering our emotions. Think of those nights when you lay in bed wrestling with an upcoming change – a wedding, a job interview, a merger, a dismissal, a doctor's prognosis. Questions abound! Where do I go from here? Who can I count on to help me get there? What actions do I need to take? Am I physically and emotionally ready for the journey? Once the four P's are understood and stored deep in that powerful brain of yours, they can be used to sift through your endless questions and ignite possible actions. They can even link those actions with group needs to sustain momentum toward success. People, Purpose, Passion, and Perseverance can be accessed as a whole, in any combination, or each P can stand alone. Applying the four P's daily will produce the best results because when the call comes for action, you will be P – Prepared.

Join us in the journey as we take a closer look at The Framework:

- People: Human Being 101 – the essence of relationships and celebration of diversity
- Purpose: The Core – the achievement of a shared meaning and intended outcomes
- Passion: The Fire Starter – the renewable fuel of momentum and the energy of leadership for life
- Perseverance: Life Happens – persistence, commitment, and why the turtle won

Reading this book won't take long, but it is only the beginning of an ongoing and rewarding personal journey. We recommend you scribble in the margins when inspired or have follow-up questions. We really believe you should journal your thoughts in whatever medium works for you. History underscores the power of self-reflection by setting context and bringing valuable focus to actions. Your reflections will pay dividends in creating your own framework for leading in life.

Once you have read this book, we encourage you to re-read, reflect, and discuss your perspectives with others because People, Purpose, Passion, and Perseverance can power an essential framework for your life and leadership.

On with the journey!

CHAPTER 1

The Framework
People, Purpose, Passion, Perseverance

High achievement always takes place in the framework of high expectation.
-*Charles Kettering*
American Inventor

Are you ready for your life to meet leadership?

The Framework equips you to unleash the power of People, Purpose, Passion, and Perseverance in that life. It is simple in design, and with deeper understanding, these four central themes work together to enrich your life and embrace your potential leadership.

People:

When we say people, we mean more than just human beings. People are the power in leadership and life. The word people is also plural, carrying with it the interactions, contributions, connections, and conflicts among a collection of individuals. Our successes and our challenges are sculpted by our relationships. How we interact in these relationships defines our organizations ... and our lives.

- The power of any organization is in its people.
- The power of those people is in their teamwork.
- The power of the teamwork is in its diversity.

Bottom Line: People make it happen!

Purpose:

Purpose is more than a goal, a target, an objective. We see purpose as the conduit for meaning and direction. Purpose makes significant the ordinary, everyday decisions in our lives. The energy, the momentum of an organization, comes from purpose.

- Meaning is the heartbeat of the organization.
- Meaning defines worthwhile work.
- Meaning opens up limitless possibilities.

Bottom Line: Purpose connects all contributions and makes every effort count!

Passion:

Passion is not mere infatuation. Passion is energy that compels people to keep going in spite of the challenges. We find our passion in the contributions we make, and individuals find inspiration in a leader's passion!

- Energy fuels momentum.
- Energy is infectious.
- Energy brings meaning to life.

Bottom Line: Passion feeds the soul!

Perseverance:

Perseverance is not working too hard, grinding away, and stepping on others to achieve our end. Perseverance is commitment. It means doing whatever it takes, rain or shine, with others and for others, to achieve a purpose. It says, "I am committed; I will be here. We are in this together."

- Commitment is to purpose.
- Commitment is for people.
- Commitment is with passion.

Bottom Line: Remember the turtle won!

Throughout the book, we have shared stories of real people who have exemplified one or more of the four P's. Some of these people are famous; most will be everyday people like you and us.

Let's begin with a reflection on a person familiar to all of us. He was born ordinary but became extraordinary when his life met leadership.

Nelson's Framework

Nelson as a young boy in South Africa listened intently to the elders' stories of the valor of his ancestors. He dreamed of making his own contribution to the struggle of his people for freedom. Working as an attorney after college, he knew he had risen to a professional status in his community, but every case reminded him of the humiliation and suffering of his people.

As Nelson grew in his convictions and activism, he was subjected to repeated bannings and various forms of repression. At first he abided by these, but quickly developed contempt for the restrictions. "I have fought against white domination, and I have fought against black domination. I have cherished the ideal of democratic and free society in which all persons live together in harmony and with equal opportunities."

Eventually arrested and convicted, Nelson spent more than twenty-seven years as political prisoner number 46664. Housed in a small cell, about the width of an average man's arm span, deprived of his family, and one of his greatest pleasures, classical music, Nelson became an inspiration to his fellow prisoners and a symbol to all those oppressed worldwide. Spurning offers for freedom if he would just renounce his position, year after year after year he held steadfast.

Released in 1990, Nelson plunged back into his life's work. Stepping into the shoes of the Presidency of an embattled democratic South Africa, he shared these thoughts at his inauguration, "We dedicate this day to all heroes and heroines in this country and the rest of the world who sacrificed in many ways ... . Let each know that for each the body, the mind and the soul have been freed to fulfill themselves."

Nelson faced many leadership challenges, but a smile creeps across his face when someone refers to his "rugby diplomacy." He first formed the idea of the political power of sport while in prison. He understood rugby to blacks was the hated symbol of apartheid. To Afrikaners it was a religion. His role as the leader was to become the father of the whole nation: to make everybody feel that he symbolized their identity and values. He set before himself the task of persuading the country to come together around the national rugby team. At the World Cup final in 1995, he felt a thrill of success when hordes of Afrikaner fans sang the Xhosa words of the new national anthem, once the symbol of black defiance.

Nelson Rolihahla Mandela accepted the Nobel Peace Prize in 1993, and has never waivered in his devotion to democracy, equality, and learning.

Nelson Mandela's story exemplifies a person who, perhaps not consciously but certainly subconsciously, lived the four P's – People, Purpose, Passion, Perseverance. On an everyday level Mandela understood the importance of relationships and how we should treat one another. He dreamed of making a contribution to his people's struggle. Well beyond that, Mandela knew people strive for dignity and will fight to maintain it or gain it.

Beyond this he kept in front of everyone the overriding purpose of freedom and dignity. Every one of his decisions – his choice to stay in prison, his selection of the rugby team as a unifying catalyst, his serving as president – all furthered the ultimate purpose for his people. What carried Mandela through all those years of struggle was the passion he exhibited and fueled in others. Passion gave him the strength, the resilience, and the will to, simply put, continue the struggle. There had to be dark times, but his heart knew his passion. Even with his people skills, his focused purpose, and his exhibited passion, he had to persevere to complete the journey. Discouragement is the enemy of perseverance and hope. Mandela had to stifle the echoes in his own mind that kept saying, it's taking too long, it's hurting my family, it's just too hard. Is it really worth it? Perseverance helped him answer yes each time.

Nelson Mandela exemplifies the use of The Framework – People, Purpose, Passion, and Perseverance – and its impact on a person and those he leads.

Leaders for Life

Each of us, like Mandela, should be the leader of our own lives; some choose to be leaders of others' lives, and many are thrust into leadership by circumstances. Being a leader in our own lives means taking responsibility for who we are and who we want to become! We know that every interaction, even the smallest, has the potential to impact others either positively or negatively. This often has a boomerang effect. We get what we give.

The more we establish a positive pattern of how we interact with others, the more others will realize this is who we are and how we "do business." Just think of the thoughts that go through your mind when you are about to ask a person to help you with a project or initiative. You automatically think of someone who has an established pattern of trust, commitment, and perseverance in the way they "do business."

When you purposely choose a path that will allow you to lead others, we think of that as front-door leadership. You accepted the call, sent in your résumé, or signed on the dotted line. You are now the leader in the organization – whether you are president of a large corporation, the chair of a church committee, or the parent of a child. You chose the leadership position.

Backdoor leadership, on the other hand, has no sign on the door. You are thrust into leadership based on need or circumstance. You accept the challenge, often without real choice. On September 11, 2001, 37 passengers on United Airlines Flight 93 were headed for San Francisco when four hijackers took control of the aircraft and diverted it toward the east coast. Todd Beamer and several other passengers instantly became leaders when they attempted to regain control of the aircraft. Life's circumstance created these backdoor leaders.

Front-door leadership will always be needed, but more and more backdoor leadership is changing the world and is the leadership most of us experience on a daily basis.

Just as true is the idea that leadership is fluid, definitely not static. Situations create opportunities to lead at one moment and follow in the next. The great leader knows when she needs to be in charge, and when she needs to be the contributor or supporter. We can learn this principle of leadership from geese. They seem to know instinctively that there will be times when they are the lead goose, and that others are there waiting to take their turn to support the flock in reaching its destination. The flock of geese is a team. Each goose is ready to take the lead position when another is tired. Each works to create the uplift for the birds that follow. Each honks encouragement. And each is even ready to drop out of the V formation to protect a fellow goose that is hurt – and protect that bird until he is ready to again join the flock. One moment a leader, the next a follower, and then back to being a leader – depending on the circumstance.

Whether you seek leadership through the front door or it finds you via the backdoor, whether it is your turn to be the leader or the contributor, The Framework will guide your journey.

Just to Keep Us on the Same Page

As you read this book and reflect on your own life and experiences, we thought it important to share our meaning of a few key terms we use throughout the book.

Our Beliefs:
Simple, Compelling, Balanced – The Three Principles That Guided Our Work with the Four P's and the Writing of This Book

* *Simple:* The architecture of the book is simple – it's easy to read; it tells the stories of real people; it affords the readers the opportunity to reflect on the four P's and apply them to their own lives.

  Simple is good.
  -Jim Henson
  American Puppetee

* *Compelling:* As The Framework is the essential driving force in our lives and our leadership, so we hope that you will be compelled by your own experiences and thinking to address the four P's plays in your life.
* *Balanced:* We must work at assuring we are strong in each of the four P's. Circumstances may demand that one of the four P's dominates the situation; life, however, requires that we keep all four P's in balance.

Our Fables:
Introduction to Each of the Four P's – People, Purpose, Passion, Perseverance

* Each chapter begins with an original fable that exemplifies one of the four P's.
* Each chapter culminates with an original wisdom, inspired by the fable and encompassing the spirit of each of the four P's.
* The fables, you will notice, come "full circle," with the final fable tying back to the first, connecting experiential wisdom.

Our Stories:
People We Have Met Along the Way

- In each of the following four chapters the reader is introduced to an individual in our lives – Scott, Grace, John, Mark – each exemplifying one of the four P's.
- The other stories and the reflections, though not as in depth, are about people in the authors' lives as well as those familiar to all of us. They are the evidence that the four P's work.

Green People:

It's not easy being green.

-Kermit the Frog

Green people are those individuals who demonstrate a pattern of being difficult, and sometimes obstinate. We all have them in our lives. We refer to them as green to remind us that they have the greatest potential for growth. It is important not to give up on them, but to nurture relationships with the green people, to change a negative into a positive, and bring them along in any organization.

Organization:

An organization is any group of people with whom you work or interact. It may be formal, an association or business, or be your bridge or book club. Your family, both immediate and extended, is an important organization. It might also be a team you are on, or a council or board on which you serve. Simply stated, an organization is a group that together shares meaning.

The Dash (–):

The dash refers to what happens between the beginning and the end. For example, 1998 – 2010: the dash is the actions, the relationships, the meaning, the energy, and the commitments that happen between those two dates. In the movie, *Hope Floats*, Birdie Pruitt reminds us that "beginnings are scary, endings are usually sad, but it's the middle that counts the most." The dash is the middle, and it does count the most. Simply put, the dash is life.

The Zen Symbol ◯ :

The Zen symbol is used by the authors to punctuate experiential wisdom and reflection. This classic symbol, the enso, is known as the circle of enlightenment. In the sixth century a text named the Shinhinmei refers to the way of Zen as a circle of vast space, lacking nothing, and nothing in excess – simple, compelling, and balanced.

Invitation to You

Leading in life and leading in your profession require the same powerful framework, a balance of people, purpose, passion, and perseverance. Continue the journey with us as we take a closer look at The Framework:

- People: Human Being 101 – the essence of relationships and celebration of diversity
- Purpose: The Core – the achievement of a shared meaning and intended outcomes
- Passion: The Fire Starter – the renewable fuel of momentum and the energy of leadership for life
- Perseverance: Life Happens – persistence, commitment, and why the turtle won

We encourage you to read the chapter that most appeals to you. There is no correct order. How you choose to read the chapters may provide insight to your own area of growth. Is it perseverance? Perhaps it is passion or purpose! Or maybe you want to start with people and delve through the chapters in the order they were written. It's up to you. Each will deepen and enrich a "down-to-earth" approach to leadership in your life.

Stop often to reflect. Allow your stories and your experiences to integrate with the ideas shared. And as you read, jot down ideas and questions in the margins. Respond to the reflective questions provided. Writing provides clarity to our fuzzy thinking. Take the opportunity to discuss your readings and new ideas with others. Let the interaction fuel your thinking and your commitment to making The Framework the essential driving force in your leadership and in your life.

All of us want to believe there is a place where dreams come true, and magic is at our fingertips to solve the challenges in our lives and assure our leadership makes a difference – for us and for those we lead. We believe The Framework of People, Purpose, Passion, and Perseverance is the magic for when life meets leadership.

Let the magic begin!

CHAPTER 2
The Framework – People

Human Being 101

I suppose leadership at one time meant muscles; but today it means getting along with people.
-Mohandas (Mahatma) Gandhi
Political Leader

Mountains Ahead

One day an old man came upon a broken-down cart loaded with bricks at the top of the mountain. Traveling soldiers, peasants, families, and artisans skirted the cart as if it were not there. "Can I help you?" asked the old man.

"I wish you could," replied the cart owner. "These bricks are needed at the foot of this mountain tomorrow evening. With the rainy season upon us, the villagers must immediately repair their flood wall. No one seems able to help me with my cart. I have failed the village below. Their bridge and fields will wash away with the next heavy rain."

The old man pondered for a moment and then spoke, "Perhaps I can help here."

"What can you do, old man?" responded the younger cart owner. "Even the strongest men on this road could not help me with this broken axle." He kicked a stone in frustration.

The old man gave him a thoughtful look. "Everyone uses the bridge when they travel this road. Perhaps you can ask the travelers going down the mountain to carry a brick with them to help the village below. I am certain that if you just ask and share your need they will understand and the goal can be accomplished. Even the heaviest of your load is manageable if you let the travelers carry what they can."

The cart owner considered the thought and then smiled in gratitude. "Thank you, kind sir. I had not considered this possibility."

The next day at the bottom of the mountain stood a heaping pile of bricks, each one carried by the travelers – the soldiers, the peasants, the families, and the artisans who passed over the village bridge.

> Give people your trust and the tools they need, and they will meet the challenge.
> *-Authors of*
> *When Life Meets*
> *Leadership*

People are the difference in where your important load of bricks lands – stranded at the top of a mountain or waiting at the bottom, where they are needed most. Every player shares a stake in the final result. Each contributes his own strength – trust, support, insight, ingenuity – to the larger group's efforts and goals. Our successes and our challenges are sculpted by our relationships. How we interact in those relationships defines our organizations ... and our lives.

Human Being 101 is based around this very concept: the power of people.

- The power of any organization is in its people.
- The power of those people is in their teamwork.
- The power of the teamwork is in its diversity.

The crux lies in how effectively people can amplify each other to achieve their potential as a team. We embrace the fact that our people don't work for us; they work with us. Everyone carries a part of our purpose forward at the moments right for her. In doing so, we rise above simply accepting differences to actually celebrating an increased energy of those differences working together. Group energy recharges every member who shares in it and reminds us of the old coffeepot that percolated when plugged in. The goal? A perfect cup of coffee. We waited impatiently at first until it began its real work. Blurp! Blurp! Blurp! Intermittently at first, but gradually it would build into a melodic and confident rhythm. Our organizations are like that. People percolate – slowly at first and then in rhythm with each other and the organization. Blurp! Blurp! Blurp! The result? An energetically percolating organization, one that consistently brews a cup worth the wait!

The skills, the talents, and even the perspectives of each team member mesh to achieve the purpose.

Does it Really Work?

In the 1940's, two men in a garage learned this valuable lesson. They recognized early on that for their growing organization to be successful they needed to encourage people working together to take risks, to be creative, to accept challenges, to be innovative, to be entrepreneurial. They envisioned the power of letting people do it, whatever it was that made a contribution to the organization and to the world. Their organization had the spirit of a large family endeavor and everyone worked for each other's success as well as their own.

This company grew out of the friendship between Bill Hewlett and Dave Packard and their can-do attitude. Two remarkable people working together resulted in an even more extraordinary organization, Hewlett-Packard. They were real human beings who worked with other real human beings. They cared about their employees. They built a company of people. They promoted the we in their organization. It was everybody's business to do a great job, working together, helping each other to achieve the extraordinary. Innovation was invited, expected, and rewarded.

During the formative years of Hewlett Packard, a universal feeling of the HP employees was that they were honored and respected. People, individuals like you and us, had the power to make decisions. Bill and Dave set the goal and then let their employees have the power to make it happen. They gave people their trust and the tools to meet the challenge, and then let those people step up, think as big as possible, take risks, and make their best contributions to achieve the goal.

If we don't connect with the energy of our team members, their potential, and even ours, is not achieved. In fact, when left uncharged for a long enough time, the team members' batteries drain. They contribute less and less and eventually produce a negative charge or, at best, no charge at all. How do you assure that the batteries of your team members are fully charged?

You Gotta Care

Scott's Story

Scott was raised on a small Iowa farm until he was sixteen, when he and his parents moved into a Midwestern community and became the neighbor of one of the authors. His dad, Leonard, worked in a construction firm with the mantra "hard work pays off." His mother, Donna, fed thousands of students over the years in the school cafeteria; Scott remembers her as someone who genuinely loved people – caring about her own family, caring about the students she served, and caring about her community until the day she died from cancer.

Hard work and caring – genuinely caring about people and their needs – are the two attributes this soon-to-retire school district worker in charge of maintenance and activities is proud to say he learned from his family. A third observable characteristic others recognize is the humbleness Scott displays when anyone praises him for his contributions to his family, the school, or the community. Scott has always been quick to point out the strengths and talents of others, and yet downplays his own personal contributions. His outlook and his actions focus his work, and without knowing it, he has a positive impact on his greater community. Patient and positive, Scott controls his environment and positively impacts others. He transforms himself to optimize his service to the organization. Everyone in Denison knows Scott and what he stands for; he walks his talk, and does it without saying a word.

Scott's impact goes beyond his work as a school custodian; he volunteers as a mentor – his first preschool mentee will graduate the same year he retires.

He is also a more-than-twenty-year volunteer for the Donna Reed Festival, a community's focus on creating opportunity for kids from the Midwest to work with show biz's famous in the performing arts. Not surprisingly Scott knows practically everyone in town and most know him. If the community or an individual is in need of anything – and Scott knows about it – he is quick to offer his assistance. Scott is definitely a positive "ripple maker"!

Whether setting up for a high school basketball game, coaching a young person, hauling pizza to feed countless volunteers, or chauffeuring Hollywood and Big Apple greats to the annual festival, Scott goes the extra mile; he makes others his priority. When asked why, he admits, "You gotta care. I just want people to be happy and my attitude can have an impact on that. Think of the bad and that is what you will get, but we really have a whole lot more positives than negatives in our lives." Scott Schurke is an example of an average man with a straightforward philosophy that guides his life: "Work hard and care about people ... everything else will take care of itself."

It did not come as any surprise when Scott was the first person selected for the community's new Wall of Pride. While he was honored for making a difference – for the quality of his work and its impact on the community – Scott sloughed it off with, "It's my job; it's what I am supposed to do. We all need to care about what we are doing – no matter what it is. And if you work with people to help them get what they need, it will all work out and we will all be happy."

Can you imagine the heights your organization might reach if you and your colleagues modeled the way Scott lives his life? What could your organization be like if you and your team had the genuine caring attitude (the glass is always at least half full!), the work ethic, and the humbleness that Scott Schurke has? Scott's secret to success is a relatively simple formula – easy to articulate but more difficult to put into action. Oh, but think about the possibilities to achieve such a wonderful life!

We want each of you as leaders to take a panoramic view of people, much like the photographer replaces the close-up lens and uses the wide view to better appreciate the breadth and depth in front of her. Look at and reflect on the entire package, the wide range of possibilities that a person can support. Initially, we tend to focus more on the skills and knowledge that each individual brings to the workplace, when actually these abilities contribute only a small percentage of what will make our organization – our business, our family, or our community – stronger.

The personalities of these team members – their values, their commitments, and the beliefs that guide and influence their behaviors – are in reality what allow us to amplify the diverse gifts and talents of each team contributor. When we use a wider lens to view each person – to understand his values of caring, her work ethic, another's spirit of collaboration and cooperation, one's patience, and that sense of humanity and humility, for instance – we can use all the qualities offered by each person and empower not only the individual but the entire team and the organization itself to accomplish great things. Yes, the people in our lives are the ultimate resource; they define the reach and the impact of who we are and can be together. This is true whether we are talking about our family or our work.

We believe in the 80/20 concept that Vilfredo Pareto, a 19th-century Italian social scientist, introduced to the world. This principle describes an apparent relationship between causes and effects.

- 80% of our monetary success in a business comes from 20% of our customers.
- 80% of the referrals a high school principal must address is with 20% of the student body.
- 80% of the work in service organizations is achieved by 20% of the volunteers.

Extending this concept, we believe that 80% of success in our lives depends on our ability to work with people and only 20% from our knowledge and skills. Think about the successful people you have met in your life – those who truly stand out in your memory. They have roughly the same knowledge and skills of 80% of those in their field, and yet they often rank among the top 20% because of their attitude, their outlook, their ability to work with and capitalize on people. They tap into and develop their potential with energized organizations because they have people power – that distinct awareness of relationships and their impact on success. These people live Human Being 101.

So what exactly is People – Human Being 101? In a family, a team, or a business, it simply is:

- Knowing and understanding people
- Cultivating genuine relationships
- Modeling the behaviors we want to see
- Capitalizing on the strengths and perspectives of each person
- Recognizing the contributions of every person

Reflection: Leading Where They Are

I have a best friend at work!

Since humans are social creatures, it is natural for them to want social interaction in their workplace. Managers who recognize this and provide opportunities for employees to develop social relationships will see the results throughout the workplace. Employees develop loyalty toward one another and this loyalty can become a deciding factor when deciding whether to stay at or leave an organization.

-Nicole T.

As leaders we must invest enough time and effort into getting to know our people, internalize their strengths and challenges, and then ensure that they have not only the tools but the confidence, environment, and support to accomplish their success together. Individuals and organizations need to get back on the right track of realizing people are the most important part of the equation.

Let's take a closer look at each of these building blocks of Human Being 101 – including a story that illustrates each.

People – Human Being 101: Knowing and Understanding People

Just how do we do that? We start at the beginning. It takes time and initiative on our part to meet people and have them meet us. When getting to know each other, it is important to share ourselves. We ask questions of each other, and we genuinely listen to the responses. Communication must be two way. We need to learn as much as we possibly can about each other. When we initiate a relationship – with this simple back and forth of being human – we grow closer and begin to relate the needs of others to ourselves. We grow reciprocally. With the investment of time in each other we emerge not only with a commitment to the goal, but more importantly, with the gift of a relationship.

These relationships need fuel. To assure that our team members are charged with energy, we must be aware of their needs. Abraham Maslow, in *A Theory of Human Motivation*, identifies the full range of basic and essential needs every person requires to move forward. We first strive to satisfy our critical biological needs – air, food, water, sleep – before we concentrate on our own security and safety. Once these needs are met, we do all we can to generate a sense of belonging through sharing our love and affection with others. Our fourth need, being valued, is achieved through self-respect and the respect

One of the oldest human needs is having someone to wonder where you are when you don't come home at night.
-Margaret Mead
American Cultural Anthropologist

WHEN LIFE MEETS LEADERSHIP

we receive from others. When this happens, we feel confident and appreciated as a person. When we sense we are not valued, we feel frustrated, inferior, and disconnected from the whole. Our responsibility as leaders is to monitor our team members, to ensure their basic needs are met so they can become and do what they were "born to do."

How Do You Inspire Others to Outperform?

Boake's Story

Boake left Dayton Hudson in 1987 as president and chief operating officer. He soon became the CEO of Revco Drug Stores, a company heading into bank-ruptcy with a $1.5 billion debt. In June, 1992, Revco successfully emerged from Chapter 11 bankruptcy. How?

He shared with us that he is driven in leadership by one central thought: "I want everyone in the organization to be as satisfied with their job as they possibly can be, so they feel they are better as a result. I want no misunderstanding; everyone must know they can do it; they are empowered to work at the top of their game and make it happen." The toughest part, he admitted, was recruiting people into a failing organization. "Have you ever wanted to work 24/7 365 days a year and leapfrog an organiza-tion into a state of art?" he asked his recruits, whom he could offer anything but high salaries. They took the jobs because they had confidence and zero fear; they believed in the dream and agreed to perform so well that their people would all push themselves to get from better to best. Boake admits that he looks for one thing in others that he sees in himself, the need to "outperform myself," to be the very best. And, he adds, "having no ego about what I don't know and being willing to learn from others."

Boake Sells, now an independent management consultant, goes on to say, "You have to give people a feeling of dignity, no matter what their role in the organization, because when you make people feel

Relationships do not power themselves.
-Authors of
When Life Meets
Leadership

less, you have lost it all." And that is exactly what you get, less. This means, of course, that as leaders we must provide time to get to know each other and then provide the tools so that individuals can do the job right. "You want their knowledge and skills to drive the business, not enable it."

So let's take a look at ourselves. What is it you do to invite people into your organization? How do you get to know and understand them? What does each aspire to be? How do you know that?

....

....

....

....

People – Human Being 101:
Cultivating Genuine Relationships

Now that we know something more about who we are in this relationship, we continue to nurture it. By showing our own vulnerabilities, we are creating an environment of trust and mutual respect. We are taking the relationship to a higher level.

People inherently want to grow commitment to each other. They seek a designated space in others' lives and specifically in the life of the organization – the family, the business, the club, the team. It is important for each of us to zero in on the passions, specific gifts, and talents that people in our lives possess. When we acknowledge that we are aware of others' strengths and contributions, we reinforce their value to the organization and this brings further meaning to the relationship.

Reflection: Grandma's Thoughts

The ease of making friends!

As a grandmother, I love to take my four-year-old grandson to the park. It doesn't take him long to spot a potential friend. He'll walk up and say, 'Hi, my name is Easton, What's yours? I have a truck; do you want to play with me?' Not even waiting for a reply, both smile, drop down in the dirt, and begin to construct roads and sand hills.

They continue to play until I call, 'Easton, it's time for us to leave.'

'See ya later,' and off he runs back to me.

I wonder how it is that small children can immediately bond by simply introducing themselves. Why is it that we as adults are so slow to trust and truly get to know each other?
-Grandma of Easton S.

Susan Scott, author of *Fierce Conversations*, advocates that "the conversation is the relationship" and that each of us builds a better relationship, a better organization, and a better world "one conversation at a time."

Get "Yeasty"

Roland's Story

At the young-of-heart age of 70, Roland set off on an adventure to navigate his 17 foot sailboat IBIS from Florida to Cape Cod on the inter-coastal waterways. Knowing the value of people and how they can enrich an experience, he invited twenty of his closest friends to join him for one-week portions of the trip.

The sky and the strong wind have moved the spirit inside me till I am carried away trembling with joy.
-Uvavnuk
Canadian Shaman

To his and his wife's amazement, nine of those friends accepted. Roland was moved by their commitment to him and to the time they would spend together.

Roland invited only "yeasty" people, ones who were very curious of mind, good listeners, risk takers, creative thinkers, and those possessing some sense of adventure! He wanted to be sure he had individuals who would not do 100% or 0% of the talking. Due to weather, water traffic, and closed bridges he understood they might wind up spending a great deal of time anchored and waiting – presenting the perfect setting for sharing thoughts, stories, and dreams.

During the 2200 mile trip, on good days Roland and his guest sailors would anchor, get gas, take in a new restaurant, and sightsee. For times when a nor'easter would shut things down, the limited quarters provided quality time for reading, discussing common interests, and expanding relationships. Roland spent great times with a mechanical engineer, a lifelong sailing partner, a consultant, another 70 year old, a reciprocal Civil War buff, and other close friends.

On June 7, 2007, eight weeks and three days from his departure in the Keys, Roland Barth reached his destination. In our interview with him, Roland shared he couldn't have and wouldn't have wanted to do it without all his volunteer "mates." In addition to the invaluable contributions they all made – relieving him at the helm, helping to raise sail and anchor, navigating – he felt these already rich relationships were immeasurably deepened and strengthened. He saw them as, "truly a gift from the sea gods."

For those of us who know Roland Barth through his many years in education as an author, consultant, and school leader, we weren't surprised that he succeeded in his sailing adventure and that he would make it a learning opportunity centered on people. After all, he is the one who pioneered The Principal's Center at Harvard University, developing school administrators and transforming the focus of their work. The Center established the message, "In education one is a learner, and, thereby, a leader." Today, Roland continues his decades of influence on education through his presentations, writings, chairmanships, and adventurous pursuits.

Again we must take a look at ourselves. Select one person in your organization – your family or your business. How might you deepen the relationship you have with this person? How will you carve out the time to make the necessary conversations happen? What evidence will you accept that the relationship is stronger, deeper than ever before because of purposeful interaction?

People – Human Being 101:
Modeling Behaviors We Want to See

Each of us plays a major role in Human Being 101. The truest way for people to take it in is to see it in action. Modeling is the greatest form of instruction. In order to develop people we must model the very behaviors we want them to exhibit.

Demonstrating Human Being 101 raises the bar for everyone. It highlights interactions and makes pursuit of effective relationships the norm. In situations that are yet to come, individuals and teams know the established patterns we have exhibited. They interact with us based on those observed behaviors.

Modeling has a subtle power. It can be positive

or negative. When people observe behaviors of others, they interpret the context and shape their own actions and outlooks accordingly. In our families, children watch each other and their parents to determine boundaries of their own behaviors. The same is true in our professional lives. Teams exhibit the same behaviors modeled and expected by the leader.

As leaders we must not only model but also acknowledge those key behaviors observed and demonstrated by others. This allows us to recognize and further develop the capacity of leadership. Our recognition of and feedback for those positive behaviors result in stronger leaders in our organization.

It's Not Easy Being Green

Jim's Story

Always expect the best from people ... and when you don't get the best, demand the best of yourself.
-Authors of
When Life Meets
Leadership

In Jim Henson's book, *It's Not Easy Being Green*, Jerry Juhl, who began working with Jim in 1961, shares that Henson "inspired people to do huge amounts of work; more work, and better work, than they thought they were capable of. And he did that by pushing himself." It was through Jim's examples, his modeling, that Jerry and the entire staff achieved beyond their own dreams.

Another of Jim's employees, Kevin Clark, shared that "mannerisms and standards of the boss trickle down" in a company. Henson "was the example and we wanted to be as creative and hardworking as he was."

Modeling the behaviors he wanted and expected became a part of everything and everyone. Each employee and the entire organization produced the highest quality in their work and created the characters they are so proud of – characters like Kermit, Elmo, and Big Bird.

Jim Henson of the Muppets was their model, their inspiration. He still is.

What are the behaviors you would like members of your team to demonstrate? And what are the specific steps you are taking to assure that they see these behaviors modeled by you? How do you provide feedback to guarantee the expected behaviors become the way the organization does business?

People – Human Being 101: Capitalizing on the Strengths and Perspectives of Each Person

The power here is recognizing the diversity in each person – and that diversity goes beyond the traditional. Work ethic has no color, compassion has no economic status, imagination has no height, and collaboration has no gender. Capitalizing and celebrating that diversity is about how success is defined and how the team taps into strengths and perspectives of individuals to make contributions in order to achieve the purpose. Richness in diversity enables us to tackle issues with a greater potential for success. Variety in perspectives helps us to see solutions to the puzzle that narrow views and approaches would miss.

Diversity means possibilities. Effective diversity amplifies itself. When we share with the team our unique differences at key moments, we add energy to attaining the final goal. Whether you carry one brick or many at once, this always means at least one less challenge standing between you and the collective goal.

Strengths are not specific to individuals alone nor are they found only in the larger team. Like a symphony, the right combination of sections – the flutes, the strings, the horns – will mix their applied talents to provide what is needed at that moment in time. These combinations will be fluid as well as moment-to-moment with members contributing when needed. "Divide and conquer" or "combine and carry" are yet other celebrations of diversity that power success.

Pay Attention to the "Soul" of Your Company

Joe's Story

For 38 years Joe worked for a shoe company, eventually reaching the position of vice-president. He uses these words to describe the culture there. "'Promotion from within' was the motto and everyone except a few specialized positions started on the selling floor. I knew the top executives and more importantly, they knew me as a person as well as an employee who could hopefully grow into a bigger role in the company. I wanted to excel at my job so that I could join those top executives and lead by their example. Unfortunately, the last three years I worked were not enjoyable; the culture changed dramatically. The leadership at the top didn't respect the veterans within the company, who they felt had been 'brainwashed' by the past. These new leaders were only interested in the bottom line. As a result, I lost respect for them." Today there is no bottom line; Edison Brothers Stores, Inc. has gone out of business.

This philosophy is too often used by some leaders: don't get to know your people; use them and then get someone fresh on board; they don't count, only the bottom line does. These leaders have no personality, don't communicate well, and generally lead by fear. Their motivational stance is that you get to keep your job. They spend very little time developing their people; instead they hire from the outside and, therefore, really don't recognize employees' contributions nor stimulate their growth. They believe turnover creates change and pay no attention to what costs –

financial, time, work culture – are involved in "getting new people up to speed."

Joe Chatman, now a successful leader with his own physical training business, believes that individuals and organizations need to get back on the right track of realizing people are the most important part of the equation. He works with clients from all walks of life – CEO's, stay-at-home moms, college professors – and strives to listen to and meet their individual needs. With his own commitment to fitness and service, Chatman models the high expectations he asks of those he trains. A client's time with Joe is reserved and stays reserved until the client chooses to leave or has met his/her goal. Even then, Joe counts these individuals as friends and valued contributors to lifelong healthy living.

Do you know and have you internalized the differences in the people with whom you work or live? Make a list of those people and then identify a strength and a perspective each brings to your organization. Is it recognizing and defining issues? Outside-the-box ideas? Gift of gab? Solving problems? Synthesizing? Communicating? Devil's advocacy? Playfulness? Whatever it is, jot it down – and then capitalize on those gifts to strengthen the individual and achieve even greater success in your organization.

People – Human Being 101:
Recognizing the Contributions of Every Person

Relationships do not power themselves. The more we invest in them, the more we enjoy in return. To keep them vital, we must mutually invest in each other. We

Celebrate what you want to see more of.
-Thomas J. Peters
American Business Author

should make people aware of what we see, value, and appreciate about their individual contributions to the whole, the shared purpose.

A recent Gallup poll revealed that 65 percent of Americans haven't received any professional recognition in the past year. A United States Department of Labor study found that the number one reason why people leave organizations is that they don't feel appreciated. We don't believe it has to be this way; recognizing and celebrating our people and their contributions are key components to motivation. Recognition is the very fabric that weaves a society together and gives individuals a sense of accomplishment and belonging.

Bernie Brillstein remembers his colleague, Jim Henson, world-renowned puppeteer and creator of the Muppets, as a person who inspired people "to be better than they thought they could be. To be more creative, more daring, more outrageous, and ultimately more successful. And he did it all without raising his voice."

You, like Henson, can develop your organization by sharing appreciation for what each person does that allows you as a team to achieve the purpose. People appreciate your feedback. They want you to be honest in providing them with information about their progress toward the shared vision. Timely, specific, and accurate feedback – both from and to you – helps the team chart success, increase momentum, and focus energies on the target. Imagine driving on a highway; your speedometer is broken, it's dusk and landmarks are difficult to see, and the faded white lines blur before you. With these limiting cues as your only feedback, it becomes much harder, almost impossible, to gauge your progress.

Formal feedback is not the only way that shows we value others. Boosting a child in a parade, opening a jar for someone with arthritic hands, or pausing in an already busy day to listen to a friend's frustrations are "everyday ways" of showing how we value people. Billy Graham, American evangelist and spiritual advisor to every President going back to Harry Truman radiated openness, sincerity, and untouchable integrity. He was quoted as saying, "I'm not an analyzer. I've got a son who analyzes everything and everybody. But I don't analyze people ... the most important thing that counts is what happens in the hearts of men." Some said he was naïve, but many more saw him as trusting, always seeing the best in people and, therefore, eliciting the best results from them. Graham's mission was not to confront but to listen and provide comfort.

Just as Graham worked with Presidents from different generations, we, too, must recognize how we work with others not in "our generation." We need to especially consider the ways we include those older and younger than we and demonstrate respect for their work, their needs, and their contributions. How do we show our value in them? With at least four generations in many of our organizations today, the answer has to be, "It depends."

The traditionalist generation, those born in the 1920's through the early 1940's, most often appreciate recognition for what they do to contribute to the work of the organization. Because they are the "silent generation," they tend to prefer your acknowledgement in writing rather than in front of a large group. The baby boomers, those born in the mid-1940's through the early '60's, are famous for contributing time – lots of it – to achieve the expectations and desire your honoring their commitment to make a difference. The "latch-key kids" born in the late '60's and '70's seek balance in their lives and often benefit from the leader's gratitude for their expertise, validation of their ideas, and the accomplishments as a result of those ideas. They seek both individual and team feedback. The Gen Y's, born in the last quarter of the 20th century, desire your recognition in understanding their needs, their uniqueness, and their specialties, interweaving their personal goals with their job performance. And then we have to remember that each person may be the "rule" of the generation they represent – or the "exception to the rule." The bottom line begs that we know, really know, the individuals in our organization, identify their contributions and needs, and show appreciation in a way that is meaningful to them!

It is important to share appreciation for others and their contributions. The return on your investment will be remarkable. How is it working for you? How do you express appreciation for individuals and the contributions they make? Is your feedback timely, specific, and accurate? Is it given in a way that is important to them?

Identify one individual that has earned your personal appreciation – for his or her efforts and contributions. Be specific in what you want to say or do to recognize those contributions. Is your message clear? Will he or she know what you truly appreciate? Are your expressions timely? Now, share your thoughts with that individual in a way that is meaningful to them.

Bottom Line:
People Make It Happen!

To paraphrase the great anthropologist, Margaret Mead, never underestimate the potential of a single human being and his or her impact on your organization. The sooner we recognize that, the power becomes ours. Regardless of what we are talking about – a business, a community, a church, a family, or even the accomplishment by a single individual of a simple task – what we have found is that the common thread of success is people. They are the power of your organization.

The Challenge

Our challenge to each of you: Internalize the power of people, step up your game in your relationships with them, and capitalize on their diverse contributions.

Zen Wisdom:
Mountains that can stand against wind and rain must yield to people with a like heart.

Reflection: Let's take a few minutes to reflect on the Power of People.

What?	So what?	Now what?
What are the key learnings and ideas I have gleaned about the power of people?	And what are the implications for my life, my business, my family?	Now what are the steps I am going to take with Human Being 101?

CHAPTER 3

The Framework – Purpose

The Core

Purpose is what gives life meaning.
-Charles H. Perhurst
American Author

Memorizing Red

One day in a small village shop, a young girl watched an apprentice feed a charcoal fire used by the metalsmith there. The man carefully placed the fuel inside the forge so that it glowed evenly with a great heat. He wiped his forehead and went outside to retrieve more charcoal.

"Why does this fire need to burn so brightly?" asked the child. She was visiting her grandfather's shop and did not even know the younger apprentice's name. The tip of the stick she played with also glowed red.

"I asked my father that same question," answered the old man as he rubbed his hands together. "He said to remember the exact color of this fire; it is important. The coals have to be red like this ripe persimmon fruit." The girl looked at him with curiosity.

"Because this is the best fire to make blades for the carpenter, the farmer, and the soldier. The carpenter needs a good adze to shape timbers for the temple. The farmer needs a good hoe to harvest radishes in the autumn. The soldier relies upon his sword to protect others in battle. All of this depends on how well my apprentice keeps this fire."

"Red like a persimmon?" came the question. "Yes, red, just so," answered the man. "If it is too hot or not hot enough, the blades will be trouble and break at the worst times. If we are not careful with our fire here, then the temple will take longer to build, the harvest will spoil, and the warrior will lose his life. Remember the red of this fire. It is important to more people than just you and me."

"Yes, I see," said the girl, concentrating on the forge again. "Red like a ripe persimmon."

As we think about the role purpose plays in our lives, more than anything else it serves as the major path for meaning and direction, just like the persimmon red fire. It makes the ordinary everyday actions and decisions in our lives significant. It reinforces why we do things in a particular manner, as opposed to how we actually try to accomplish things.

Reflection: Leading Where They Are

A woman with a purpose

I want to make an intentional impact on others. I want people to be better having known me ... . I'm definitely nobody's Oprah. But a kind word, a smile, some advice, a ride home, lunch on me, or just an ear. I want to help others become better than they are without compromising who they are.

-Tambi G.

Our lives are literally filled with small, even minor, tasks and interactions. If, however, they all are somehow intertwined with a greater purpose, the meaning and satisfaction we feel are more powerful. We think of a single thread as but a strand, but threads woven and intertwined form a blanket. As a blanket, those threads retain heat; this is a blanket's purpose. Acting as a unified whole, the blanket fulfills a need that the individual threads, acting alone, could not. Each must do its job with and for the collective.

Acting as a unified whole is just as important in our families. Every young couple as they begin to rear their first child is concerned about their new responsibilities – the child's health, safety, and education, all of the "stuff" of everyday life. However, if you were to ask the parents, "What is your hope for this child?" the answer goes to a much deeper meaning. "To be the best person she can possibly be, even better than us, her parents!" The everyday "stuff," combined with a greater purpose, creates a stronger future for their child. Each succeeding generation, therefore, has the potential to surpass the previous one.

In the world of business, the same concept can be utilized. Leaders who are mindful of their everyday interactions have an advantage as they work to unite their colleagues. It goes beyond vision, mission, and goals and produces a greater whole! It asks the simple question, "What is it we ultimately want to accomplish?" It certainly is more than an initiative or a project, and ideally it leaves a lasting legacy – in our organizations, our families, and our lives!

The energy, the momentum, of an organization comes from purpose.

- Meaning is the heartbeat of the organization.
- Meaning defines worthwhile work.
- Meaning opens up limitless possibilities.

Above all, everyone needs to understand his/her relationship to the purpose, and must consistently revisit it to stay in touch. What direction do we best serve? How do we keep purpose out in front of us? Do we go adrift when the leader is not present? Wouldn't it be something if individuals came with a little "beep" or light that flashes if they run counter to their or their organization's purpose? Staying on the right track should be so easy, when, truthfully, it is often fraught with wrong turns, detours, and backtracks!

Many men go fishing all of their lives without knowing it is not fish they are after.
-Henry David Thoreau
American Philosopher

Actually, when you live your purpose, others will experience it through their interactions and relationship with you. It might be said, "We are living examples of our purpose!"

Does it really work?

Just thinking of George Bailey in *It's a Wonderful Life* should bring to your mind the idea of purpose. If you've seen it, you know; if you haven't, do yourself a favor and rent it. It's a classic with repeated airings on television through at least the last four decades. The movie revolves around George's life as a small town savings and loan manager. Even though he had big dreams of traveling the world and being adventurous, he is stuck in Bedford Falls due to multiple circumstances.

On Christmas Eve, George believes he is ruined because of the loss of $8000 due on a loan. He sees his life as having been a waste and he decides to end it all by jumping off a bridge. An unlikely angel, Clarence, seeking to earn his wings, saves George. Clarence shows George through a series of flashbacks what life would have been like if he had never been born. It's a "wonderful" way to see how even the smallest events can touch and enhance the lives of those around him. George realizes the treasures he has and the choices he can make go way beyond money. George must choose which treasures mean the most in the end – for himself, his family, and his community. The moral of the story is simple: all of us leave a legacy; it's our choice what it is!

Establishing a positive culture is one of the essential cornerstones of purpose. It serves to bind individuals to the "work." They feel comfortable, respected, and they want to contribute. In our daily lives there are countless opportunities to connect, disconnect, and reconnect. We can easily lose sight of our ultimate purpose. These insignificant distractions have a tendency to drain us both mentally and physically. Through these times, focusing on our purpose and working in or living in a positive culture give us the energy and stamina to look forward to waking up each day to continue the journey. Purpose is the sustaining force.

Even nature knows the value of individual and collective purposes. When people see shimmering heart-shaped golden leaves blowing in the wind on a cold Western mountainside, they know they are enjoying the Aspens. These trees grow naturally in stands with many atop the same expanding root colony. Their collective purpose is to maintain the mountainside – protecting against erosion, resisting attacks by pests or fire, and providing 500 different creatures a wildlife habitat. While trekkers on the mountain may simply appreciate the brilliant autumn foliage, the Aspens are fulfilling their ultimate purpose, preserving the mountain and its wildlife.

So what exactly is Purpose? Simply put, it is The Core:

*   Knowing and understanding the ultimate intent
*   Communicating consistently and constantly that intent
*   Connecting people and resources to make it happen
*   Each staying true to the purpose

Grace's Purpose

What Did She Do When Life Happened?

Through a happen-stance meeting at the Des Moines airport, Grace was introduced to the authors. We learned immediately, if there is a magnetic north to Grace's life, it comes from knowing at a young age that she loved taking care of others, being useful, and meeting life's challenges tenaciously. Whenever she swung away from her chosen path, she would patiently find ways to work back into alignment with her personal compass of purpose and happiness.

Grace's parents sought out the promise of California from their native Japan over 100 years ago. They were educated in law and home economics but had to reinvent themselves to face the realities of their new home. Born near San Francisco, Grace worked with her siblings to help support the family with food, shelter, and basic needs after her father suddenly passed away in 1930. What little she had left from her summer farm earnings, she saved for college, a fundamental family value and expected life goal.

Grace had known she wanted to be a nurse since

All endings are also beginnings. We just don't know it at the time.

-Mitch Albom
American Author

she was eight years old. Her love of taking care of others even extended to her dolls. She was full of life, excelling at athletics and school academics. By 1938, she entered the pre-nursing program at the University of California at Berkeley. She had just started at the School of Nursing when the United States entered World War II in 1941. Presidential Executive Order 9066 cut short her nursing education by relocating her family to an internment camp at Gila River, Arizona.

When Grace talks to students about this event, she sets it in context the way she and her future husband, Minoru ("Min") Amemiya, experienced it. "You can start life by only what you can carry in two suitcases," she notes, "but it's hard to lose your citizenship when you feel deeply your own American pride." She worked as a camp nurse aide while she was incarcerated for a year. Like other Japanese American nursing students, she sought other avenues of education to complete her coursework, but many institutions returned letters of rejection for her situation. She finally was accepted at St. Mary's School of Nursing in Rochester, Minnesota, in 1943. With it, she was also able to join the U.S. Cadet Nurse Corps of the United States Public Health Service. While stationed in Iowa, she served returning servicemen at Schick General Army Hospital.

Grace's outlook on life reflects more of these experiences. She said plainly, "Treat others as you want to be treated yourself." Her sense of care was vastly broadened by the life of her first son, Michael. Born with health defects and seizures, he was not expected to live or develop beyond a few short months. Faced with decisions of what to do, Grace and her husband took it on faith they should accept the challenge and Michael thrived well into his 40's, surprising many specialists who had had their doubts. She even became an ardent community volunteer of the Special Olympics in Iowa, a contribution she was recognized for in 2010.

She reflects humbly on such recognition and sees

the awesomeness of people throughout her life. Her husband passed away from a brain aneurysm, yet she was with him to the end, holding his hand and talking to him with a caring connection of life's purpose and sense of shared history. She laughs easily with enthusiasm for the here and now, the present day (especially for anything related to sports!)

Even history has healed some of its ways for Grace. In 2009, after she addressed the University of California Board of Regents, they unanimously voted to award honorary degrees to survivors of the internment who were denied their original opportunity for degrees. Their diplomas bear a special Latin inscription that reaffirms "to restore justice among the groves of the academe."

In listening to the stories of Aiko "Grace" Obata Amemiya, she has no bitterness, only optimism for working things out. "In camp, we helped each other out, we coped, we did what we had to do," she said, even if it went against cultural traditions and norms. "You have got to be yourself," she continued, touching again her own internal magnetic north.

The building blocks that were evident in Grace's life are also evident in others and can be in yours. Let's take a closer look.

Purpose – The Core:
Knowing and Understanding the Ultimate Intent

When you have a keen interest in something, it is a strong motivator – so is the desire to learn and grow. Link these and you create purpose and success in those you are leading. Og Mandino, the author of *The Greatest Salesman in the World*, recognized that successful people "take on their own lives ... by charting or consciously choosing their desired destination and the path to reach it."

The more intensely we feel about a goal or idea the more power it sends to action. Your purpose may be oriented toward the family, your career, or even toward yourself. Our lives do move in and out of passages due to time, age or circumstances. Knowing where we want to go or what it is we ultimately want to accomplish gives us guideposts to move through, and better yet, capitalize on those journeys.

Literature abounds with the concept of "loving self and others" as an ultimate purpose, and there certainly is some truth to that strain of thought. Leo Buscaglia was teaching in the Department of Special Education at the University of Southern California in the late 1960's when one of his students committed suicide. She had been one of the sets of "kind eye-balls" he always looked for in the large auditorium because her responses showed him at least one student was hearing what he said. The news that she had killed herself had a great impact on him. He voiced, "What are we doing stuffing facts into people and forgetting that they are human beings?"

Buscaglia created a non-credit class titled *Love 1A* and became a cheerleader for life. "Life is a banquet," he would say and "most poor fools are starving to death." Through books, presentations, and television, he was most closely associated with the topic of love and human relationships, emphasizing the value of positive human touch, especially hugs. He wrote, "It's not enough to have lived. We should determine to live for something. May I suggest that it be creating joy for others, sharing what we have for the betterment of person-kind, bringing hope to the lost and love to the lonely. Only you will be able to discover your uniqueness, and when you do, it's your duty to 'give it away.'"

He always said, "I really didn't 'teach' the class. I facilitated it – helping the students to discover their own magic. We are all born with God-given, unique traits and skills. But, as with all possibilities, they will remain unrealized unless they are developed, nurtured,

I am here for a purpose and that purpose is to grow into a mountain not to shrink to a grain of sand. Henceforth will I apply ALL my efforts to become the highest mountain of all and I will strain my potential until it cries for mercy.
-Og Mandino
American Author

and put into practice. You may have the 'capacity' to love, but if left undeveloped, you will never gain the 'ability.'"

Daniel Pink, author of *A Whole New Mind* and *Drive*, emphasizes the concept of knowing yourself as an individual. He wrote, "Lawyers. Accountants. Computer programmers. That's what our parents encouraged us to become when we grew up. But Mom and Dad were wrong. The future belongs to a very different kind of person with a very different kind of mind." Pink goes on to ask each of us to identify "our sentence." Some would say Abraham Lincoln's sentence, his purpose, was to save the Union and free the slaves, "A house divided against itself cannot stand. I believe this government cannot endure permanently half-slave and half-free." Winston Churchill's sentence, or purpose, was to inspire fortitude in a World War, "Victory—victory at all costs, victory in spite of all terror, victory however long and hard the road may be; for without victory there is no survival." Helen Keller's sentence was to show that people with disabilities could learn and live with dignity, "Never bend your head. Always hold it high. Look the world straight in the eye." Hopefully you know your sentence, your purpose, and better yet so do others.

However, even when we know our sentence, our ultimate purpose, life may intervene and the timetable we planned has to be put on hold.

What Is the Only Thing You Have Ever Wanted to Do?

Joanne's Story

Joanne was born in 1965 in Yate, Gloucestershire, England. As a child Joanne often wrote fantasy stories for her sister. She recalled, "I can still remember me telling her a story in which she fell down a rabbit hole and was fed strawberries by the rabbit family inside it." When Joanne was a teenager, her great aunt "who taught classics and approved of a thirst for knowledge, even of a questionable kind," gave her an old copy of a book written by Jessica Mitford. Mitford became Joanne's heroin; she read every one of her books. As she moved through school and into college, Joanne's parents wanted her to earn a vocational degree. However, her parents had hardly departed from campus that first day before Joanne went straight to switch her studies to the classics. She did not blame her parents for their stance as they had experienced poverty, and they wanted better for their daughter. A degree in the classics was certainly not viewed as a path to a good life.

After her studies, Joanne moved to London to work as a researcher and bilingual secretary at Amnesty International. In 1990, while she was sitting on a delayed train ride to London, the idea for a story started forming in her mind. It involved a young boy attending a school of wizardry. She later told reporters, "I really don't know where the idea came from. It started with Harry, then all these characters and situations came flooding into my mind." When she reached her destination, Joanne began to write, but her life was about to change and Harry would have to wait.

In that same year, her mother died, and shortly after Joanne moved to Portugal where she met and married a television journalist. They had one child and divorced in less than a year. JK, as she had been called most of her life, moved to Scotland to be close to her sister. She went back to school and finished her first novel – on an old manual typewriter while living on state welfare. Initially the manuscript was rejected by twelve publishing houses. The decision by Bloomsbury to publish actually hinged on the opinion of Bloombury's eight-year-old daughter who was given the first chapter to review and immediately demanded the rest of the story. In 1995, Harry Potter and the Philosopher's Stone was printed with an initial print-run of 1000 copies. Harry Potter is now a global brand worth an estimated fifteen billion dollars. The series has been translated, in whole or part, into 65 languages.

While addressing a graduating class at Harvard, JK Rowlings said, "Half my lifetime ago, I was striking an uneasy balance between the ambition I had for myself, and what those closest to me expected of me." She went on to say, "I was convinced that the only thing I wanted to do, ever, was to write novels."

What's your purpose? Let's take a look at ourselves. What evidence can you present that your time and efforts directly contribute to the fulfillment of your purpose? What actions signal to others, in your family or work, that you know your purpose? What values do you hold that support that purpose? Can you identify your "sentence, your purpose"?

Purpose – The Core:
Communicating Consistently and Constantly the Ultimate Intent

This one is fun – it's the opportunity to paint the picture – let your imagination and creativity reign. You can use broad, colorful strokes or quiet, contemplative words. Just be sure it taps into the heart of each person and strengthens the heartbeat of the family or business. Purpose thrives and grows in an atmosphere of openness. You cannot share the intent too much or too often. If you had access to satisfaction surveys given by companies, you would see that communication consistently surfaces as an area for needed improvement. Individuals want it to be faster, more often, in greater depth, written, or even delivered in person! What is really important is that all our communications reinforce the connection to purpose.

Purpose uncovers meaning!
-Authors of
When Life Meets
Leadership

A leader's vision isn't worth much if it doesn't reach the intended target. And even if it does achieve its aim, it won't go far without ongoing effective communication. Purpose has to be shared in order to inspire action. Consistent and constant communication of purpose reinforces dedication, shared values, and common hope. Great leaders don't wait for formal processes to connect with employees. They are out there asking for suggestions, discussing concerns, and enlisting buy-in. Further, they instill a sense of trust; this is especially true in a family, where actions build a cushion of support for growing and learning. It is the leader's responsibility to really listen to needs and remove the roadblocks so individuals, families, and teams can effectively fulfill their personal as well as the organization's purpose.

Based on surveys given by Sirota Intelligence to about 1.2 million individuals at Fortune 1000 Companies, the majority of employees are very enthusiastic when they start a new job. However, in approximately 85% of those companies, employee morale sharply declines after the first six months. Most companies simply do not continually place before their employees a strong, clear mission – one that says to them each day, this is why we are glad you are here and this is how your actions contribute to our purpose.

Communication does not have to be elaborate. Take the story of the Nordstrom department stores. For more than one hundred years Nordstrom employees have known and communicated the organization's purpose. John W. Nordstrom established the business in 1901 on exceptional service, selection, quality and value. Today, Nordstrom has grown from one downtown Seattle shoe store into a nationwide fashion specialty chain with renowned service, generous size ranges and a selection of the finest apparel, shoes and accessories for the entire family.

For many years, new employees were given a copy of the famous Nordstrom's Employee Handbook – a single 5" x 8" card.

Nordstrom Rules

Welcome to Nordstrom. We're glad to have you with our company. Our number one goal is to provide outstanding service. Set both your personal and professional goals high. We have great confidence in your ability to achieve them.

Rule #1: Use best judgment in all situations.

There will be no additional rules. Please feel free to ask your department manager or division manager any question at any time.

Today workers do get an actual handbook, but Nordstrom, Inc., has been repeatedly listed in Fortune Magazine's "100 Best Companies to Work For." They were one of the first companies to embrace the idea of corporate social responsibility. They make every effort to run an ethical business where people want to work and shop. They believe it is just good business. Social responsibility efforts help Nordstrom connect with customers and employees and help drive results. As the card says, every employee can make an on-the-spot decision to meet the customer's need. Need this skirt altered? Let me call alterations for you. Need a package mailed? Of course, give me the address. Need a different size? I'll be glad to call another store. What hasn't changed over the years? The company's living purpose: offer the customer the best possible service, selection, quality and value.

One proven way to keep purpose alive is to tell a good story. Relatives love to reminisce at family reunions about the sacrifices and risks their great-grandparents took to build a better life for themselves and their future generations. Employees at the annual meeting often recall the time they worked all night to reach their goal. Stories create trust, capture hearts, and pique interest. The story binds us to the purpose. Terrance Gargiulo, an international speaker and organizational development consultant, says it this way, "Stories catapult our imaginations into new directions. Many of our habitual ways of looking at things can be altered by a story's capacity to engage us. Our connection to others and our understanding of their perspectives is deepened by a story's ability to inform us in ways that words themselves cannot do."

What's your purpose? Let's take a look at ourselves. How do you consistently communicate your or your organization's purpose? Could people you interact with or lead voice or explain the purpose in which they are involved? Would they feel your actions tell a story of purpose?

Purpose – The Core:
Connecting People and Resources to Make It Happen

You must be the change you wish to see in the world.
-Mahatma Gandhi
Spiritual and Political Leader

Most people want to know they are making a difference! With the changing American family, economic hardships, increasing demands on our time, and the complexity of life in general, we long for a sense of control and a feeling that our actions are worthwhile. Unfortunately, many individuals just walk through life relying on their automatic pilot, hoping that it will get them from Point A to Point B. They neither recognize nor seize opportunities to generate a better or more fulfilling life for themselves, their loved ones, or their peers along the way.

Seizing opportunities can relate to time, money, people or expertise. Actually, we all have the same amount of time each day, but individuals who know their purpose use directed time. They weed out tantalizing distractions knowing the goal cannot be accomplished with watered-down commitment. Another word we seem to have lost in today's hectic pace is "No!" The call comes to us with the mantra, "You're the only one for the job!" or "We always know we can count on you." Each of us has to be strong enough to value our own time and how it will be used. Granted, at work, it is not always our option to say no, but a good leader will be very aware of his/her staff's workload and will protect their productive time frame.

When the word resource is posed to most people their minds turn immediately to dollars. "How much is it going to cost?" "Who's going to pay for this?" Certainly valid questions for any project or initiative, but the concept of dollars, and what those dollars can teach us about maximizing resources, goes much deeper. Whether the money you might have is a dollar or thousands of dollars, the object is to see it grow so its potential can be maximized. By making consistent deposits and with the benefit of added interest you can establish a strong financial base. However, that's not to say it is easy to wait for the effect of contributions on the whole. Deposits certainly make a positive difference in the end, but it's like putting together a jigsaw puzzle one piece at a time – the end goal is only slowly built up, but it is satisfying to see fragments of the final goal emerge around the edges. The same is true in life and work, our weekly deposits with the added benefit of staying true to purpose yield a greater personal and collective worth.

People and expertise are almost synonymous. Unless you are a robot or a computer you will need people and their specific knowledge or skills. Well, actually, today you still need a person to design and program robots and computers, but for us as leaders this goes right back to "Human Being 101." Except in

Creativity is the power to connect the seemingly unconnected.
-William Plomer
South African Author

this case, you are working to connect the right person with the right job or the right team with the right project. You arrange it so they have the other two resources – time and money. You make sure they know the intended purpose and have the skills to complete the project – then you "turn them loose." Soon you'll be congratulating them on what a tremendous job they did.

Are There Hurdles to Your Purpose?

Lori's Story

Born in 1982, Lori came into the world with scant resources and a family with few roots. She attended eight schools in eight years and watched her single mother take multiple jobs to support the family of six. One year as they prepared to move again, Lori told her mother, "Mom, I can't go to a city that doesn't have a track. I'm trying to pursue my dream."

Bring out the best in others!

-Authors of When Life Meets Leadership

After striking out on her own as a young high schooler, Lori had to rely on others to help connect her to resources that would foster her goal. For the very basic need of survival, others saw great potential, drive, and commitment in Lori, and they took her in. She actually lived with four different families during her high school years. Qualifying for financial aid, Jones went on to Louisiana State University and competed on the track team. Her coach, Dennis Shaver, was a mainstay for her with his expertise and support. In 2004 when Lori failed to qualify for the Summer Olympics in Athens, she was demoralized and told him she wanted to retire. He simply said, "I'll see you at practice tomorrow." Despite her second thoughts, Jones knew her heart was in running – and always had been. So without major sponsorships she tackled multiple part-time jobs to earn money to leave the country for competitions. Coach Shaver continued to back her and even told big-time sponsors, "Her day will come if given the opportunity."

Working her way back up through the track rankings by leaning on her LSU surrogate family, Lori finally garnered sponsorships from Nike, then Asics. For the first time in her life she had the resources and tools other elite athletes used to maintain peak condition. She went on to win her first national championship in 2007 and numerous other meets in Europe and the USA. Then came the 2008 Olympics in China where she was touted as the person to beat; instead she became known as the "girl who was leading the race when she tripped and fell."

After China, Lori really had to regroup to stay true to her purpose, because every time she was introduced at an event they would replay the video of her stumbling with the gold medal within her grasp. She simply said, "You know they're not going to forget it; I'm not going to forget it. I can't be sour about what happened. I can only look at the positive side of it." One of the unexpected positives was the public's reaction to how graciously Lori handled her defeat with the whole world watching. People even sent e-mails to Asics, her shoe and equipment sponsor, saying how much Lori's behavior had inspired them. Asics never wavered in their support.

"Lolo Jones is a great American story. You don't get that many anymore, with people who grew up poor and seize every opportunity. And she really did," said Randy Essex, whose family was one of the ones who welcomed Lori, now more famous as Lolo, into their home.

Lolo would be the first to recognize that she would not be who she is today nor have accomplished all she has without the support of individuals and organizations that believed in her. Each of us has a responsibility to make a difference in the lives of others.

Oprah's Angel Network is an example of such an organization. One of the officers, Gregg Sherkin, describes it this way, "The concept of community has been forever changed. No longer simply a group of people who live close to each other, we can define community as a group of like-minded people, possibly on different sides of the globe, who share common beliefs, values and goals. I have traveled to just about every region of the world and met some truly inspiring people who have helped me understand the reality of what it means to be a part of a 'community' in the world we live in today.

"I've witnessed the pain a mother in Africa feels when she loses a child to disease, and it's no different from what a mother in this country feels when she experiences that same loss. When I asked a child at a school in Soweto what she wants to do when she grows up her answer was the same as that of a child I spoke to at a school on the southwest side of Chicago. They both said, 'I want to be a doctor.' Not only do these people share common experiences and goals, but they have the potential to support each other to achieve their dreams, if provided with the right tools and the motivation to use them.

"My firsthand experience has shown me that the dream and desire for a better future is a common goal that is not bounded by geographical borders. It's the access to resources that really separates us."

Let's take a look at ourselves. Have you taken stock of your resources and how they are being used to support the purpose? As a leader, how do you consciously make decisions that maximize the connections between people and resources? How do you overcome the hurdles that are placed in front of your purpose?

Purpose – The Core:
Staying True to the Purpose

At the beginning of an initiative when the purpose has been made clear, resources have been allotted, and excitement is high, it is easy to stay the course. It's when the setbacks arrive and the luster of hard work has dimmed that "staying the course" becomes difficult. Celebrating along the way highlights movement toward the purpose, recognizes individual and group contributions, and provides an excellent opportunity to say again "We're all in this together." People hunger for signs of progress. We don't always have to have our leaders or parents tell us when we're making progress – we should be trusted, at times, to see that for ourselves. We get anxious if we don't have some degree of personal participation and control.

Celebrate what you want to see more of.
-Thomas J. Peters
American Business Author

By connecting with purpose we gain unlimited promise. These possibilities are generated by each of the participants who are aware of, understand, and subscribe to the purpose. A wise leader harnesses and celebrates the energy that has passed from member to member. Recognition does not have to be big and overt; it can be as simple as a pat on the back, a line in the newsletter, or a simple acknowledgement like "We're proud of you." Actually taking a break to connect or celebrate successes along the way can push a large project further on down the conveyor belt or spark a round of creativity. Humans are masters at "piggy backing" on others' ideas. Celebrating is a wonderful excuse to draw colleagues together and use their collective thoughts and efforts.

Oh, if life could just be about celebrations, but we all know there are many zigzags, detours, and course corrections in our journey through life or our career. Most of us have to take stock and constantly readjust; otherwise, it is just too easy to get off track and entirely miss our purpose. Good leaders help people through those course corrections; great leaders anticipate and work with their teams to devise contingency plans.

Daniel Webster, a famous orator, once shared during a heated debate in the United States Congress, "Mr. President, when the mariner has been tossed about for many days in thick weather on an unknown sea, he naturally avails himself of the first pause in the storm, the earliest glance of the sun to take his latitude and ascertain how far the elements have driven him from his true course. Let us imitate this prudence and before we float on the waves of this debate refer to the point from which we departed, that we may at least be able to conjecture where we now are."

Early sailors obtained their bearings by using a sextant. This instrument enabled men to measure the angular distance of the sun or the stars from the horizon, in finding the position of a ship. Those who failed to look up and make needed course corrections often perished, whereas the wise mariner who used the sextant in fixing position usually reached his safe harbor.

The storms of life can easily drive us into unknown waters. Therefore, from time to time we, too, must get our bearings, and discover how far we have been driven from our true course. That certainly doesn't mean you can't change directions; just be sure the new direction is leading you to your intended destination.

How Do You Bring Out the Best in Others?

Dale's Story

Sometimes you have to be a bulldog!
-Authors of When Life Meets Leadership

Dale's purpose in life was developing people – people in his family, his community, and his church. He managed to earn a living and honor his purpose through multiple avenues, needed course corrections, and enlightened initiatives.

Dale's first job was for the Ford Motor Company, and he was quickly offered a promotion. He and his wife had grown to love their hometown in the Midwest, and wanted to raise their three children there, so he turned down the position. He then began a long career at a limestone company, where he became their treasurer and eventually vice president. After his retirement from that company, he took a completely different path and became an assistant funeral director, which brought him great joy. He told everyone, "It was the work he was meant to do."

Throughout his life, Dale was a beacon for the development of the community. Wanting to assure quality of life for those who lived in "his" community, he served as a team member and mentor of fellow Jaycees, the City Council, and the commissioners of planning and zoning. The community recognized Dale in 1996 as Citizen of the Year for his vision and impact on people and the community.

His sense of purpose rippled throughout the greater community. As an avid runner, he loved athletics and was an Official of the Drake Relays, serving several times as its marshal and always a model of purpose. He was inducted into the Drake Relays Hall of Fame and helped found the Corporate Relays.

Faith was the center of Dale's life, and he and his wife, Kay, were instrumental in establishing the Gloria Dei Lutheran Church, where he served in a multitude of elected and volunteer positions. Dale, like others we have shared, did whatever it took to make it happen. It might be a kind word, a needed dollar, or hours of labor – all to achieve his purpose of developing people.

Dale Readinger always gave his best, and when he died of cancer, he left behind a stronger family, church, and community. All because, as his family wrote in the tribute for his funeral, "Life's gifts are your legacy to us. Through your life, we learned the essential lessons of life."

What's your purpose? Let's take a look at ourselves. How do you or your organization take time to celebrate positive steps toward your purpose? What course corrections have you chosen to stay true to your purpose? Are you willing to be a bulldog to achieve your purpose and further the purpose of others?

Bottom Line:
Purpose Connects All Contributions and Makes Every Effort Count

Purpose gives life meaning. It is the whatever-it-takes effort of individuals toward the purpose that makes the difference.

The Challenge

Our challenge to each of you: Identify your purpose. Then do whatever it takes! With the charged terminal of purpose, Your Framework has meaning.

Zen Wisdom:
Leave winter cold and summer heat outside when building a perfect fire for your forge.

Reflection: Let's take a few minutes to reflect on the Power of Purpose.

What?	So what?	Now what?
What did I learn about the role of purpose?	*And what are the implications for my life, my business, my family?*	*Now what are the steps I am going to take with my core – the purpose?*

CHAPTER 4
The Framework – Passion
The Fire Starter

*People achieve greatness when they act
from their hearts and their passion.*
-**Benjamin Disraeli**
British Prime Minister

Smile Anew

One day at the edge of a lake, a group of weavers carrying fabrics to market arrived at a small ferry with a lone operator. After they stepped aboard the boat, the old man pushed away from the shore and began to row slowly across the smooth water.

A traveler asked the ferryman how long he had worked on the lake. "A very long time," he said without missing a stroke. "I cannot even count the number of trips now."

"How are you able to make so many trips year after year?" asked another young weaver. "How can you live without even seeing beyond the mountains of this lake?"

The rower smiled as he pulled on his oar. "Every trip is new to me. My passengers change. The trees and flowers change. The seasons and crops change. The families and children change. Even the wind and currents change with each trip. At night the moon keeps me company and even she changes with the sky full of stars."

He smiled broadly as the boat approached the far bank with its waiting customers for the return trip. "Everyday I meet someone new and I learn what lies behind the mountains and beyond." He slowed the boat gently until it bumped the shore. "I look forward to enjoying the beauties of this lake just as you enjoy the beauties at your loom," he said to the young weaver. "I barely notice the rowing that I do because the time passes so quickly."

The young weaver was the last to leave the boat. She paid her fare and left the ferryman with a delicious dumpling that she carried with her. "Thank you," she said, adjusting her load. "Your smile has been the biggest change for me. I now know the secret of its warmth," she said, returning the smile.

Passion is like a miracle resource that can be unlimited and give us increased energy, more happiness, and a stronger connection to the people we touch. Passion, however, is not perpetual unless we feed and nurture it. The key is to tap into that resource to establish a boundless supply. It's taking the time to search our hearts and minds for what triggers us personally in our lives. Passion will get us up and going in the morning and color our dreams with joy each night. It is knowing who we want to be and how we want to impact life.

Passion is the fire burning in all of us. It is the fire starter making everything we do worthwhile. Passion is the energy feeding our soul.

- Energy fuels momentum.
- Energy is infectious.
- Energy brings meaning to life.

Reflection: Leading Where They Are

Struggling to find my passion!

Going to work each day was a struggle – getting through the day was a battle. Had I lost my passion?

I found that I simply lost sight of what was important. I was too concerned with how good I was as a teacher – getting frustrated that I was not being recognized for the work that I was doing. In the long run, I realized that recognition was not what was most important, rather that my students were learning and excited about learning was more important. The passion was never lost, just hidden – buried deep among unimportant junk.

-Sarah K.

It's obvious when people are operating from passion. They are focused – 100% focused – and they don't let obstacles stand in their way. With renewed energy fueled by their passion they reframe challenges, refocus purpose, and reenlist others to the cause. The confidence they exude spreads to everyone with whom they work. The surest way for passion to be contagious develops when our core values, beliefs and actions match those with whom we work or live. Passion definitely has a ripple effect.

It is too easy to let life's daily demands rob us of our passion. The dog has to be groomed, the kids have to be at practice at five, the board wants the report by tomorrow, and you are struggling to please everyone. Stop long enough to reconnect with your inner passion. Know you will be a better you to everyone, including yourself, when you take time to reflect on and renew this resource. Think about an activity when time just seemed to fly; you were so engaged in the process that rather than getting bored or tired, you were recharged to achieve the goal. Each of us needs to know what triggers that invigoration. It might be play for one, study for another; others may find renewal of their passion in needed rest or even attacking a challenge. The important thing is that when your passion needs rekindled, you know how to re-ignite that energy.

Passion also gives us permission to fail on our way to success – to take risks. We accept mistakes, learn from them, and move forward. Passion is what allows us to live the life we deserve and smoothes out the bumps in our journey. It creates and carries priority.

And with that priority comes the responsibility to fuel the passionate energies of others. All people come with fuel cells. Circumstances determine whether those cells are switched on or off. As leaders, we create the environment that supports the ignition of passion.

Don't ask yourself what the world needs – ask yourself what makes you come alive, and then go do it. Because what the world needs is people who have come alive.
-Howard Thurman
American Philosopher

John's Passions

Intersecting Passions Connect People

As a child, John discovered an image in his grandfather's office that would change his life forever. It was a dynamic pencil sketch of steam locomotives drawn by his uncle that set fire to this little boy's imagination. Like the passengers of that train, John embarked on an exciting journey that would reveal to him and affirm for us the power of passionate living.

John's fascination with trains grew outward in a quest to see that magical drawing move. His creativity poured into drawing, painting, photography, reading, and study of film and animation.

Then came the summer of 1977 – the heroes of *Star Wars* assembled to see their destiny fly by them in a wire-frame computer simulation of the Death Star trench attack. John didn't know how (home computers were in their infancy then), but he would have to find a way to bring that medium into his dreams as well.

"Today's Internet didn't exist back then. We did things the human way – by word of mouth, reading, trial and error, intuitive association, and simple blind luck." What he was looking for was hard to find because it was still being invented and recognizable only to a few. A prominent computer science professor even suggested that he turn back to study other computer theory – there was no real future in computer graphics or movie making. The path that John was on seemed only visible to him. And every visit to his grandparents meant that the train drawing patiently reassured John's vision.

His tireless quest ultimately led to his long-time participation and leadership of ACM SIGGRAPH, a technical and educational society of computer graphics that helped pioneer much of what we take for granted today. His animation work ended up on a variety of videos and a feature at the Smithsonian Institution. He even animated an interactive steam passenger train on the world's fastest graphics super-computer of 1997. A circle was complete for him, and yet far from finished.

"I have learned that an important part of passion-ate living for me is people. Connecting and learning from them constantly inspires me with possibilities, even if our passions differ." When John energizes you, like he did us, with his feelings about passion, he invites you in to a center of his beliefs. "Passion is one of the most honest relationships you can have with yourself and others, especially yourself," he beams. He sees passion as an essential ingredient and mirror for living. It is a state of being that requires care, feeding, and sharing.

"People might think that passion is an outcome, like a pursuit or hobby. I feel it is more of a reservoir that we fill and re-fill with the combined energy of our life interests. When we spend passionate energy on an important interest to us, we are really restoring a whole lot of other things necessary for a fulfilling and joyful outlook on our life ahead."

John pondered this further with us. "In one way, passion is a form of trust we have and use. When it engages us, we have freedom to make discoveries, mistakes, achievements, and disappointments for ourselves. It is sometimes permission, sometimes cour-age. Whatever it is for you, I think we collect it, share it, and respond to it in others when we have experi-enced it ourselves. That is where the fun really begins."

"When it comes right down to it, we actually share very common intensities when we set aside our judg-ments of how different passions are expressed." Find-ing commonalities and connections are important themes when you get drawn into a conversation with John. "Well, we have certainly witnessed a world that would sometimes like to decide your differences for you. We need to go beyond the cover of the book. In the context of life and leadership, we need to know that the best kind of possibilities happen when people can volunteer their passionate energies at the right time and place for us all."

To this very day, John appreciates these notions – and so do we as we witness his passion. He knows that his eclectic interests and experiences are like scattered dots that he happily connects around him to make real differences. More importantly, he hopes that others are doing the same. "I feel that passionate living spills over into everything around us – that is why it is important to encourage it in all our endeavors. Like my uncle's train drawing for me, it is the spark that gives. The benefits are huge, especially for the whole."

For John, passion extends to the horizon. "Passion is actually part of a greater continuum for me. It sustains part of the life spirit that takes care of the long future in front of us. I feel this is where our differences will count the most. Differences that amplify each other – together."

So what are the building blocks of Passion – the Fire Starter? Simply said, they are:

- Knowing and understanding passion comes in different forms.
- Fueling passion to achieve purpose.
- Celebrating the excitement that passion contributes.

Let's take a closer look at each of the building blocks that fuel John's passion and can be the fire starter of yours.

The Fire Starter:
Knowing and Understanding Passion Comes in Different Forms

Since passion is so individual, we need to celebrate the passions of others, and respect their choices. When you ask most people to identify a person with passion, they describe a charismatic individual who lights up the room; people who have a glint in their eye, an excitement in their voice, rapid speech, and expressive hand gestures. However, when we start to reframe how we look at people, we become so much more aware of all individuals and their different facets and gifts. Take the librarian who is usually quiet and contemplative with a book close at hand and ready to say "shh" any moment, who positively lights up when you ask her about a certain topic or recently published children's selection. The quiet demeanor can mask a deep and heartfelt passion.

Tapping into a person's passion can only be accomplished by spending time with that person. Relationship building is much more than just listening. It means focusing on the other person long enough to truly hear the words she says, and key into the energy and feelings exhibited. In some cultures they translate this as "I see you!" Once you identify the person's passion you can reaffirm it, tap into it, or foster its re-ignition.

Of course, knowing your own passion and trans-mitting that message in multiple ways to everyone is just as important. It also means one of the leader's passions should be in leading people. It takes a caring and knowledgeable individual to inspire others and enlist their desire to further the purpose of the organization.

You can't fake true passion; as a leader you must be genuine – the passion has to be transparent and ring true in every action. If you laugh, enjoy your day, radiate fun and show sincerity, you help keep the energy level around you at its peak. People don't just listen to what you say; they watch to see if actions match your words. People want to work for someone who inspires them to be better!

Amazingly, all of us gain when we appreciate others' passions – without judgment. People express their passion in different ways. One person's passion may burn with an open flame, obvious to all. Others' passions are like slow-burning embers – smoldering underneath but ready to ignite when fanned. Our job is to uncover those passions, to seek clarity in

A great leader's courage to fulfill his vision comes from passion, not position.

-John Maxwell
American Author

understanding each, to support individuals in their commitment to their passions, and then to focus those passions toward a common purpose.

Paul Newman demonstrated this kind of passion – true, not fake; energized by others and their needs; and expressed in many forms.

The blue-eyed screen idol for more than 50 years, Newman was described in *Paul and Me* by his pal and playwright, A.E. Hotchner, as the "same man in 2008 that he was in 1955, unchanged despite all the honors and the fame, not a whisper of change." Passions drove his life.

Paul's first evident passion was drama. He began his studies in acting at Kenyon College, a private liberal arts school in Gambier, Ohio, after an athletic injury ended his sports career. His on-screen debut was in television, quickly followed by Broadway and motion pictures. Not all were successful, and yet he continued to hone his craft, fuel this passion. His roles as Rocky Graziano in *Somebody Up There Likes Me* and "Fast" Eddie Felson in the *The Hustler* earned him fame and fortune early on. They also taught him to develop his characters in the real world, hanging out at a gym to polish his fighter antics and playing pool with shark Willie Mosconi. Fifty movies, nine Academy Award nominations, one Oscar for best actor in *The Color of Money*, and numerous other awards are evidence of his passion for his career.

His commitment to acting and development of aspiring actors in the business resulted in formation of First Artists, a production company co-founded with Barbra Streisand, Sidney Poitier and Steve McQueen, assuring performers the opportunity to produce their own projects, to fuel their own passions.

Newman's passions didn't stop with acting; another was his love for racing. He thrived on pushing himself to go faster, make sharper turns, win more races. He admitted he started slow. Like acting, it took him a while to get into it, to know his part, to make it "organic, a part of me." Just like his movie characters

Passion is the source of our finest moments.
-**Joss Whedon**
American Screenwriter and Producer

Hud, Butch, Luke, and Rocky materialized over time through Newman's interactions with people in the real world, P.L. Newman, the racer, emerged as one of professional racers' own and with a national championship in 1976. "It was like getting four Oscars with wheels," he said. Racing remained a passion throughout his life. At age 75 he was still competing at Daytona, going 185 miles an hour. Now that is letting passion drive your life.

Newman's successes went beyond the world of acting and racing. He was driven by his passions for people and their success – whether it be social activism, actors' creative rights, the arts or his philanthropy. His competitive drive evidenced in the movies and on the track was the intrinsic value that fueled these other passions. You could count on him supporting the things he cared about.

Committed to social activism, Newman was a vocal supporter of the civil rights movement. In 1968, he and his wife, Joanne Woodward, campaigned full time for Eugene McCarthy. In honor of his son who died of an accidental drug overdose, the Newmans established the anti-drug Scott Newman Foundation. They also formed The Hole in the Wall Gang Camp for children with cancer and other blood disorders.

He was a man made uncomfortable by compliments, a man who preferred criticism because he felt it was always sincere. In the same way, his passions were often exhibited behind the scenes. He didn't like what he called "noisy philanthropy." His contributions were often anonymous. Whether it was daily visits with Jim, the ailing jack-of-all-trades who helped Joanne and Paul with major projects around their home, or coaching kids in acting camp back at his alma mater, his love for people and their well being was a priority.

Newman's Own, a food company, was co-founded by Paul and his long-time friend Hotchner and fueled by Newman's love for his culinary skills and helping people. Among his family and friends, he was the master chef of hamburgers and salad dressing, spaghetti sauce and popcorn, and even lemonade. These have been the mainstay of Newman's Own and have resulted in more than $300 million donated to charity, all post-tax profits and royalties earned by Newman in the company. Thousands of charities across the world have benefited from these donations. Tens of thousands of individuals continue to reap his support – kids at cancer camps, the homeless trained to have and sustain self-resiliency, and countless unknown through the Canary Foundation, an organization dedicated to research in technology for early detection of cancer.

In Hotchner's words, Paul Newman was "a complicated, unpredictable, talented man who certainly gave back to the world as much as the world gave to him." His daughters shared that their father was "a rare symbol of selfless humility, the last to acknowledge what he was doing was special. Intensely private, he quietly succeeded beyond measure in impacting the lives of so many with his generosity."

His passions fueled his life – and those of others he touched.

How do your passions fuel your life, and the lives of others?

The Fire Starter:
Fueling Passion to Achieve Purpose

It seems obvious to us that people who love their work or what they are doing enjoy it much more – they are passionate about it. Through passion they find their purpose and their meaning. They become committed not only to their individual success, but to the organization and those around them. This is the ripple effect passion has!

Passionate people get more done because they spend less time worrying. They share their passion and lift others around them. They aren't looking for ways to get out of work; rather they take the initiative to move forward. They certainly aren't clock-watchers. They are too busy being excited about purpose and the time they can devote to achieving success.

Space Story

Sally Ride, the first American woman in space, created a life for herself based on her passion. She worked to obtain Bachelor's and Master's degrees and eventually a PhD in astrophysics. After reading an ad in the Stanford University paper, she knew she wanted to be an astronaut. More than 8,000 men and women answered that same ad, but Sally was selected and went on to serve as the communications officer on the second and third flights of the Columbia.

Above all, be true to yourself, and if you cannot put your heart in it, take yourself out.
-Author Unknown

Sally Ride was and is a role model for women. She demonstrates daily that if you really want to do something you can, no matter what. Ride helped change our society for women and influenced one woman in particular.

Just as Sally always knew her passion, another young girl was sure of hers. When Mae Jemison's kindergarten teacher asked her, "What do you want to be when you grow up?" Mae replied: "A scientist." Her teacher said, "Don't you mean a nurse?" Mae shared her thoughts. "There is nothing wrong with being a nurse, but that's not what I wanted to be." Jemison did become a scientist, earning a degree in chemical engineering from Stanford. She also earned a Doctor of Medicine and served as a physician in the Peace Corps.

After Sally's experience in space in 1983, Jemison felt the astronaut program had opened up and she applied. As one of the Mission Specialists on STS-47 in 1992, Mae became the first African-American woman to orbit the earth. "The first thing I saw from space was Chicago, my hometown," said Jemison. "It was such a significant moment because since I was a little girl I had always assumed I would go into space." Passion fueled her purpose.

Both women eventually resigned from NASA, but each went on to establish their own companies and engage in motivating kids, especially girls and young women, to excel in math and science. Dr. Jemison established a foundation in honor of her mother; one of the on-going projects of the foundation is an international science camp where students work to solve current global problems. Dr. Ride is chair of the Deloitte & Touche Council on the advancement of women. "Females are 50% of the population and we cannot afford not to tap into that group of people to the fullest extent possible," Dr. Ride told BBC News. Naturally both women have received numerous awards and honors!

When a student in an interview asked, "Do you have a motto?" Jemison quickly replied, "Purpose." Putting together her passion and purpose, Jemison remembers, "I felt like I belonged in space. I realized I would feel comfortable anywhere in the universe – because I belonged to and was part of it, as much as any star, planet, asteroid, comet or nebula."

Sally's dad simply encouraged her to reach for the stars, and she did – literally!

Passion knows no color, gender or time bar-rier. It can capture, fuel and propel anyone to great heights! Just as Ride and Jemison overcame societal barriers to fulfill their goals, Ma Li triumphed over her own physical challenges to not only fulfill her passion for dance but instill it in another.

Ma Li's Story

Ma Li, a promising 19-year-old professional ballerina, lost her right arm in a car accident in 1996. Wanting at first to just give up – the same reaction many of us would have, she forced herself to become an independent person – learning how to write again, brush her hair, and even take care of her home.

In 2001, with passion in her heart, she returned to the theater and met her life partner, Tao. They worked together in the performance arts until 2004 when China closed all the theaters. Devastated and with no money, this young couple huddled in an underpass, waiting for a new day, a new beginning. It was there as they danced in the snow that they realized the next steps in their life of performance.

Ma Li and Tao by happenstance ran into Zhai Xiaowei, a 21-year-old Special Olympics cyclist who had lost his leg in a tractor accident when he was four years old. His athleticism and optimism coupled with a sense of humor and a can-do attitude gave him the courage to accept Tao and Ma Li's invitation to become Ma Li's dance partner. Intensive training and practice day in and day out for a year, beginning at 8:00 A.M. and never ending before 11:00 P.M., allowed them to overcome the challenges and difficulties (Zhai dropped her more than 1000 times!) that most of us would never endure.

Ma Li and Zhai Xiaowei were the first handicapped couple ever to enter the national dance competition on Chinese Central TV (CCTV). They won the hearts of millions through their compelling testimony of the power of the human spirit, recognizing that with perseverance and passion people can do anything.

So let's take a look at ourselves. At this moment, how passionate are you? About what? Have you shared this passion with others? How? Does your passion for your profession fuel your life? Or does your passion for life fuel your profession? How are they ignited by each other?

The Fire Starter:
Celebrating the Excitement that Passion Contributes

Passion speaks its own language – sometimes subtle, sometimes loud and noisy, but always necessary. Passion is a fuel! It is a positive influence on everyone it touches. Successful leaders of an organization exude passion. Exhibiting passion infuses everyone in the organization with energy and an I-want-to-be-part-of-it spirit. It calls each of us to renewed action and a sense of team. Passion creates energy – energy creates more passion! More ripples!

When you are working with passionate people, the conversation naturally rises above the ordinary. It is more compelling and is elevated by excitement and enthusiasm. Suddenly everything has new meaning to you, and you get caught up in something you feel is worth your time and energy. People resonate with passion.

Those passions become the conduits to talk, share, and dream about the organization's purpose. It is through these interactions that we can identify and design ways to harness individuals' talents and gifts to achieve that purpose. When we recognize and reaffirm each other's passions we set forth a great multiplier of energy, human talents, and potential. Simply said, it's the snowball effect. Through this very process of recognizing and reaffirming, we are celebrating each person's passion and their unique contributions to the organization's success.

Our society is not quick to celebrate. We are much too busy thinking and worrying about what went wrong or what needs to be accomplished to take the time to rejoice in the positive. And yet a celebration becomes a true snowball. It gives you the reason to have fun, to get hooked again on life, to re-engage, and share all of this with others.

Blake's Story

Blake launched five successful companies before the age of 30; however, this was not to be his most amazing feat in his relatively young life. It wasn't until he befriended children in Argentina that his greatest challenge and greatest triumph would come together. While there, he witnessed literally thousands of children who had no shoes, making them susceptible to a debilitating and disfiguring disease caused by walking barefoot in silica-rich soil. Touched and determined, he had an idea of how he might help. With the support of family and friends, Blake took on what to most seemed like an impossible challenge, finding a way to build a company that could, indeed, put the shoes on the feet of all children needing them.

There are only two ways to live your life. One is as though nothing is a miracle. The other is as though everything is a miracle.
-Albert Einstein
American Genius

His business model was simple, a one-for-one model. For each pair of shoes sold in the conventional way, another would be given away for a child that had none. Using this innovative business approach, Blake felt he might have a chance of not only giving away shoes periodically, but if, indeed, the model was successful, the company could be an on-going benefactor.

At first many people laughed at Blake, but he was determined to "beat the system" and prove good people united by purpose and passion might change the world, one step at a time. His first job was to hire amazing people, people so passionate that his vision became theirs. Together they did whatever it took to make the seemingly impossible a reality.

Blake knew that the company would need to make a quality shoe that would have a higher price point than the average ... but he hoped that the message behind the purchase of every shoe would make the difference to his customers. Shortly after starting the company Blake was back in Argentina giving away 50 pairs of shoes to those children that had none.

The next time Blake returned to Argentina he had 17 friends and family members along with him. This was his first big "shoe drop," as they fitted shoes for 10,000 children and their families. Just the logistics associated with the fitting of the shoes was daunting, but the emotions felt by the team members were unexpected and powerful. A close friend and partner of Blake said this: "You need to enjoy your life. I am working and have no money ... but I am enjoying life!" The volunteers who helped Blake described the event as "amazing, overwhelming, too much ... and necessary!" This drop also doubled the education of many Argentinean children as they no longer had to share shoes every other day in order to walk the miles to school.

Blake's passion was indeed "rippling"!

More than ever, Blake and his team felt the call to work smarter in order to truly become that "benefactor company." The initial "shoe drop" was a spiritual experience for all, but now was the time to kick it in gear and be all they could be. They had promised the people in the villages of Argentina "they would return."

They celebrated their initial successes and used that energy to build an even larger and stronger company. TOMS Shoes was officially in business to stay! The TOMS workers believe that "this is what we are supposed to be doing," giving of themselves to be one world. They continue their quest because simply there are millions of children still needing shoes.

TOMS Shoes began with a distribution of 50 pairs; in September of 2010, they gave away their 1,000,000th pair. TOMS Shoes and its founder, Blake Mycoskie, have also been recognized by the State Department's Award for Corporate Excellence. The ripple continues as the model has expanded to providing eye glasses as well as shoes.

Passion really can "catch fire" and ultimately change the world ... one step at a time!

So are we having fun yet? Is the passion making a difference? What has been the ripple effect of the shared passion? How do you celebrate that passion?

....

....

....

....

....

Bottom Line:
Passion Feeds the Soul!

Passion is what makes you jump out of bed in the morning ready for a new day and new experiences. People without passion for their work and their lives live only for their vacations and weekends. Unfortunately, they may be missing out on the happiness of everyday life. When your work, your life, and your passions all become one, everything is meaningful – and even fun.

Find your passion. Let it lead you. Let it be you!

The Challenge

Our challenge to each of you: Internalize the power of passion, step up your game in fueling your own passion – and others', and capitalize on passion as it fuels your life. With the charged terminal of Passion, you have strengthened Your Framework and are doing what you love.

 Zen Wisdom:
Beware of the returning smile that cannot stay hidden – it betrays a passion!

Reflection: Let's take a few minutes to reflect on the Power of Passion.

What?	So what?	Now what?
What have I learned about the power of passion?	So what are the implications for my life, my work, my family?	Now what are the steps I am going to take to renew the passion – the fire starter?

CHAPTER 5

The Framework – Perseverance

Life Happens

Knowing is not enough; we must apply.
Willing is not enough; we must do.

-Johann Wolfgang von Goethe
German Philosopher

Rivers Behind

One day along a crowded mountain road, a family came upon a man with a broken-down cart. He was returning to the village near the river below.

"Can we help you?" asked the mother. "Oh, yes," said the young man, "my cart is broken down and others have helped by carrying these bricks to repair the floodwall below. If you can carry a brick with you, I would be very grateful. We must protect the village before the next rain."

"I want to help," volunteered the little boy. "We live in the village below," said the father, "and I can carry a few." The boy pleaded again to help. "Only if you carry it the entire way," cautioned the mother. The boy nodded eagerly. "Thank you so much," said the cart owner, bowing with gratitude.

Some time later, the boy dropped his brick on the road. "I am too tired," he cried. "We are all tired," said the mother, "but this is very important."

The mother crouched down before the boy. "You must carry your brick all the way to the bridge. You promised the man that you could. If you leave it here perhaps there will be a hole left in the wall that the water will pour through. Our home might then wash away." The boy understood his promise as he lifted the brick from the road again. "Your arms will tire less if you carry it this way," offered the father with his own bricks cradled to his chest.

Late that afternoon, the family reached the river bridge and found a waiting cart filled with bricks. With a tired smile, the boy added his brick to the pile. "Our wall can be finished now," said the little boy.

That night in his warm bed, he dreamed of a wall with no holes.

Perseverance is the mortar that holds together the other bricks in the wall. It is also the adhesive that has the tendency to lose its bonding power. People often give up before they achieve the needed change or impact they desire.

Think of all the diets so many of us have tried and yet still failed to accomplish our goal. We start with the clear purpose of being healthy and in shape; we have the passion to struggle through the expectations of the diet – all the rabbit food and water – to reach the ideal. We even surround ourselves with the people who can coach and support us toward our purpose. All is going well and then life happens and we lose our focus. Our ideal is lost; we return to our old ways, and our past practice of eating any and everything again becomes the norm. What was missing? Perseverance – our willingness and fortitude to "hang in there" to realize the ideal.

Perseverance is really where we spend most of our time in leadership – and life – if our purpose is to survive the test of time. Mentioned earlier, the dash refers to what happens between the beginning and the end. Sometimes the dash denotes an entire life of an individual, for example, 1948-2007; other times it illustrates a short span of time, as with an initiative or project. Think about the dashes on your résumé. It is the steady progress that must occur between the start and the finish if we are to be successful in accomplishing our intention. We cannot stop at the end of our first wind. Just like marathon runners, we must have a fueling plan that takes us the duration of the race and assures that we don't crash on empty because we overshot our reserves.

Steven Wright, American comedian, actor, and writer, reminds us that "Hard work pays off in the future; laziness pays off now." Perseverance is what gets us through the dash and to that future. While it may not get us there today, we are closer than we were yesterday. Our talents and skills may be ordinary, but we can attain anything with extraordinary

Perseverance is more than strength and endurance. It is also about realism. Is it smart to cross Death Valley without a canteen? A bucket? A water truck?

What is the right balance?

-Authors of
When Life Meets
Leadership

perseverance. Even Albert Einstein admitted, "It's not that I'm so smart; it's just that I stay with problems longer." Perseverance allows us to grasp our dreams.

A Japanese proverb tells us that when we fall seven times, we must stand up eight. Failure is the path of least persistence. How willing are you to keep on trying – to stand up eight times?

Mark's Perseverance

Do You Have the Backbone to Be Resilient?

As a young man growing up in the Midwest on the family farm amongst close-knit family and friends, including one of the authors, Mark was pretty much a normal American boy. Up through high school he had his share of "pushing the limits" on behavior, was smart but didn't always apply himself, and was a good athlete.

On February 23, 1997, life happened! Everything changed when Mark and his younger brother were unloading a truck used by the family for hauling plywood. Ten sheets of that plywood fell on Mark, forcing his C3 vertebra out of line, jerking away his spinal cord, instantly rendering him a quadriplegic. He was life-flighted to Des Moines where his family and friends surrounded him with love and encouragement.

Mark quickly realized he had some pretty tough decisions to make about his life – one of which was where to get rehabilitation. After deliberating, Mark chose Craig Hospital in Denver, Colorado, where he found strong support for his physical and mental needs. He had to explain to others how to dress him, help him gain access to his computer, take care of his catheter, and basically how to assure he was breathing minute to minute. He was looking at life in a wheelchair – not news a sixteen-year-old kid expects or wants to hear.

Fighting depression was one of Mark's fiercest battles. He knew golf was gone, driving was gone, and football was gone. He had to plan everything – eating, waking, sleeping, and bathing – all things the rest of us take for granted. He found himself asking the question, "Do I kill myself ... or move forward?" He realized before he chose death that he had much more than most individuals in his circumstance; he had insurance, a community, a home and even a van that was accessible ... and above all else, an incredible circle of family and friends who loved him. They wanted Mark in their lives!

Next on Mark's decision screen was his education. He chose to return to his home high school and stay for his junior and senior years. Without the assets of mobile legs and arms, he needed to figure out what he did have. Mark was a smart young man so he decided he wanted to go to college. He was accepted and studied software engineering for two years at Iowa State University. Hating the cold weather, and with the help of his older brother, who was a nurse, he moved to Arizona and pursued his studies.

During his three years in Arizona, Mark found a new caregiver, Sheila. She was engaged at the time, but the two of them could not deny the attraction they had to one another. Eventually Sheila broke off her engagement, and she and Mark began a relationship. By then Mark had taken a strong interest in the law and was accepted at UCLA. Mark loved it there; he said the energy was amazing. Shelia went off to Hawaii to finish her degree and his family was back in Iowa, so Mark faced huge challenges without his usual support system. But Mark was no quitter!

At the party following his law school graduation, in homage to their unconventional relationship, Sheila got down on one knee and asked Mark to marry her. He said yes. In July, Mark took the bar in California, where the passage rate is the lowest in the nation. In November, while on their honeymoon in Hawaii, Mark and Sheila learned that he had, indeed, passed the California bar exam. What an over-comer!

Mark says friends would now describe him as just that, an over-comer – triumphant and a bit argumentative, as he never turns down a debate – but also loving and caring. Sheila describes Mark as compassionate, passionate, and generous. Others would say that upon first meeting Mark it takes about five seconds before you no longer see a wheelchair, you just see a man. A man who makes everyone feel at ease in his presence.

Mark has persevered through so many barriers in his young life and yet he gifts joy and passion for life to all with whom he comes into contact.

Mark and Sheila Willets recently embarked on a journey around the world. Both have put their careers on hold and are having the experience of a lifetime! Oh, what wonderful challenges are ahead for this amazing young couple – and all achieved through their perseverance to live life their way!

Mark's fight was not just to overcome the result of his accident. He had to pull his will and psyche back into shape and choose to go on. That is the miracle of perseverance. It's stored inside all of us. We simply need to tap into it and use it!

Perseverance for Mark and all of us is based on the concept of commitment.

- Commitment to purpose.
- Commitment for people.
- Commitment with passion.

Reflection: Leading Where They Are

Finding I can make it!

Perseverance is the key to moving forward and making a change! I have learned this concept well in my personal life. Having gone through my divorce and realizing that I was going to make it on my own – this truly takes persever-ance every single day and putting one foot in front of the other!

-Rachel R.

Perseverance through the dash, our collective journey, is interdependent with people, purpose, and passion. For perseverance to even have a chance it requires meaningful work; work that draws us to do whatever is necessary. Perseverance is what takes us through the dash – from the start of our purpose to its finish. It is about choice and action, passion and people, purpose and perseverance. It is not just waiting or passing time.

It is with passion that we persevere. Jim Henson, worldwide renowned puppeteer and creator of the Muppets, summed up the impact of passion and perseverance on purpose when he said, "If you care about what you do and work hard at it, there isn't anything you can't do if you want to." Thomas Edison echoed this same connection with his famous quote, "Genius is one percent inspiration and ninety-nine percent perspiration."

Perseverance is key to leadership and relationships. The people whom we lead – whether our families, our teammates, or our business colleagues – want to know we are with them for the time it takes to accomplish what we say is important to the group. We are the ones who create the sense of challenge and provide the tools and supports to achieve that change. Trust is key. Those we lead want positive relationships with us that make them feel they are not alone in accomplishing this goal. Our trust fuels their hope in seeing their own progress, in being able to persevere themselves through the dash. Leaders remind their team to tap into their own commitment, alignment, and dedication to the shared goal. Leaders encourage groups to find ways to give and take from each other so that the group carries itself. It is more than guidance; it's helping to keep the ties among people fresh, lively, and reliable. Peter Drucker, management consultant and self-described "social ecologist," reminds us "Organizations are no longer built on force. They are increasingly built on trust ... this presupposes that people understand one another.

Taking relationship responsibility is therefore an absolute necessity. It is a duty."

And a must if we want people to commit, to persevere, toward the purpose.

So what exactly is perseverance? In a family, a team, an organization and most importantly in you, it simply is:

- Knowing and understanding what commitment means.
- Cultivating a sense of certainty that together we can do this.
- Just doing it! Taking action!
- Celebrating the evidence of the progress.

As leaders we must invest time to achieve our purpose and we should do it with passion to achieve the trust and support of the people in our lives to make it happen.

Let's take a close look at each of the building blocks of perseverance.

Perseverance:
Knowing and Understanding What Commitment Means

In Search of Character, a training component for all age students developed by Elkind + Sweet Communications, Inc., in association with Character Counts, seeks to help them identify the benefits they derive by being diligent, getting them to think about how to be diligent, and inspiring them to be more diligent than they already are. They ask students to reflect on their commitment to doing their best, always striving for excellence; their willingness to risk failure for a worthwhile goal; the level of their self-discipline; their learnings from their mistakes and failures; their long-term commitment to the big picture; and their focus on goals. They also ask them to evaluate their level of commitment as it is related to giving up or

Diligence – the mother of good luck.
-Benjamin Franklin
Founding Father

procrastinating. Where would you score yourself as you reflect on those characteristics of individuals who are diligent and commit to the long haul?

Very few people achieve anything great without commitment, without first dealing with obstacles. Lee Iacocca, American CEO known for his revival of the Chrysler Corporation in the 1980's and now author of *Where Have all the Leaders Gone?* reminds us ... there ain't no free lunches in this country. And don't go spending your whole life commiserating that you got the raw deal. You've got to say, I think that if I keep working at this and want it bad enough I can have it. It's called perseverance." That, friends, is commitment – whatever it takes to make it happen, your willingness to be there for the long haul. Perseverance.

Vincent Freeman, played by Ethan Hawke in the movie, *Gattaca*, demonstrates the impact of perseverance in one's life. He is a love child, a child born out of wedlock and, thus, without the family history and culture that often impact our work and our achievements. This young man wants to be an astronaut but because of his background he is not considered ideal subject matter for the role. He, however, continues to prepare, to study, to exercise, to take risks, but always losing to the success of his "perfect" brother.

He finally challenges this brother to a race in the ocean, swimming out as far as one can go with the loser being the first to turn back toward shore. Vincent's success in the race becomes the turning point in his life. He explains his success to his baffled brother, "I didn't save anything for the trip back." He was prepared to die in order to win. "There is no gene for the human spirit." His commitment was revealed in his willingness to risk everything, even his life, to achieve his goal. For him, there was no turning back toward shore.

Identify a commitment you have made and kept – to yourself or to others. What role did your human spirit play? What were the steps you took to assure the commitment? What were the challenges or barriers you overcame? Why? How? What have been the positive results of that commitment? You have just defined what commitment means to you.

Perseverance: Cultivating a Sense of Certainty That Together WE Can Do This

As leaders, we recognize we cannot achieve our purpose without people, without a team working together, taking responsibility for putting the puzzle together, one piece at a time. To do that, we must develop the capacity of our people to take ownership and to become partners in exploring the unknown, testing the waters, and completing the journey.

That partnership has to be built on trust and mutual respect. Your team depends on you. The environment you create must assure these individuals feel secure to take risks. They need to know that when their experiences are saying, "Give up," you are right there with them sharing hope and encouragement with, "Give it another try." You are the voice of perseverance, reminding them of the stonecutter who hammered away at the rock a hundred times without even a crack, and yet split the rock on the very next blow.

Being a leader is a full-time job. One of our most important tasks in assuring perseverance for the work we want accomplished is providing the tools and supports to achieve the expectations. Some of those tools include clarity in the expectations and the resources to assure realization and sustainability of the purpose. No one, except by chance, has ever achieved a purpose without the clear definition of expectations and the resources of time, people, money, and expertise.

A timeframe for the job allows people to parcel their own time, to complete the tasks within the deadlines. It takes well-budgeted money to achieve the shared goal; the job is to assure the allocation enables achievement. Expertise from outside as well as inside our organization can keep us on the right track.

Assuring the right people on the team is a resource we often overlook. Our most important job as the leader is to know our people. Dr. Morris Massey, producer of training videos in management and human relations, reminds us, "If you truly want to be effective in today's world, if you sincerely want to understand other people, it seems absolutely critical that we accept the reality that all these people out there who are different from the way we are, are just as right, correct, and normal as us." And often just as scared as we are to enter into new relationships, new partnerships, and new work.

Therefore, part of our responsibility is developing our team's capacity to produce at their best in our organization. The first and most important step is getting to know them. We cannot make assumptions about them – or if we do, we must at the very least test those assumptions. We need to know them beyond their knowledge and skills; we need to really know them. We gain by teasing out their attitudes and aspirations for this effort and their lives. And we need to provide clarity in the behaviors we want exemplified. Only when we have that clear picture is it fair to delegate the work we want accomplished. By knowing our people, we will be able to provide the supports they need to accomplish the goal – knowledge for some, skill for others, and inspiration for all.

Another focus of our responsibility must be sharing our passion for the work and for the people doing the work. As leaders, we reaffirm that this is the right path and that we will be there to see it through with them, always developing their skills and their dreams to make it happen. Initiatives and programs do not change people. Your relationships change people.

Always Skate Toward the Goal

Herb's Story

Herb's obituary reads that he lived a life "that inspired others to achieve their dreams." His forté was turning around sports programs – many of which "finished last" before he arrived on the scene.

He was an innovator, a self-driven man, whose success was attributed to his ability to motivate others, getting the most out of them to achieve their goal. He coached the University of Minnesota's Golden Gophers to three NCAA championships; he led St. Cloud State University to become a Division I school. He played on two Olympic teams and coached three, besides several professional teams.

His players have identified "Brookisms" that tell the story of his own persistence and his ability to motivate them to go the extra mile to assure the dash in their lives was what they wanted it to be: "You can't be common, the common man goes nowhere; you have to be uncommon." "Boys, I'm asking you to go to the well again." "Write your own book instead of reading someone else's book about success."

His most famous speech included these words: "Great moments are born from great opportunity. And that's what you have here tonight, boys. That's what you've earned here, tonight. One game. If we played 'em ten times, they might win nine. But not this game. Not tonight. Tonight, we skate with 'em. Tonight, we stay with 'em, and we shut them down because we can! Tonight, we are the greatest hockey team in the world. You were born to be hockey players – every one of ya. And you were meant to be here tonight. This is your time!! Now go out there and take it!"

Herb Brooks coached the 1980 USA *Miracle on Ice* hockey team, a squad of college kids, who overcame the powerful USSR team and earned the first American Olympic gold medal in hockey since 1960.

We agree with their coach who said, "Willie Wonka said it best: we are the makers of dreams ... ."

So let's take a look at ourselves and our team. What is it you do and say as the maker of dreams? How do your team members know you are committed to the purpose? To them? And with passion? What approaches do you use to ignite their commitment?

Perseverance:
Just Doing It! Taking Action!

Difficult things take a long time, impossible things a littler longer.
-Author Unknown

Earl Nightingale, motivational writer and author, reminded us more than 50 years ago not to "let the fear of the time it will take to accomplish something stand in the way of your doing it. The time will pass anyway; we might just as well put that passing time to the best possible use." Those wise words guide us not only to plan, but more important, to put that plan into action.

As leaders work through the dash of an initiative they certainly will encounter barriers. These obstacles come in all shapes, sizes, and personalities. The leader needs to anticipate these potential roadblocks and have personal strategies to work through them. Perseverance!

Three of the more frequent roadblocks to success are green people, Life Happens! and procrastination.

Green People:
We All Have Them!

For many years in describing difficult people we have used the term "green people." This was long before green referred to the environmental movement.

For us, green people are those individuals in our lives, both personal and professional, who create a pattern of negativity. While many of us choose to just avoid them, we see them as young green sprigs with the most potential to grow! So how do we nurture these individuals?

The first step is to get to know them – truly know them. This takes time up front but reaps benefits in the long term. In establishing deeper and more positive relationships with these green people, we must display a genuine interest in them. What are their passions? Who are the people in their lives? What drives them?

Reflection: Enter the Green People

Making positive contacts!

I began to honestly realize that I had become a situational people avoider.

I know now that I can no longer do that. I have decided to make only positive contact with these green people, keep my standards clicked up, and model the type of behavior that I expect of myself and them.

My goal is to build trust and open communications.
-Ted H.

Second, we avoid the temptation to put up with the negative patterns of the past. We capitalize on what we have just learned about them to match their strengths with the roles and opportunities in the organization. As leaders, we should emphasize clarity in their role and its importance in making a difference in the organization.

The third step, often overlooked by leaders, is to use recognition, not so much as a reward, but as a strategy to continuously and consistently affirm an appreciation for their growth and positive contributions.

Taking the time to know each team member

builds the individual while simultaneously strengthening the whole.

Life Happens: Playing the Hand You Are Dealt

Life happens! is all the "other stuff" that interrupts or changes the course of our days. It can be as mundane as dead batteries, heavy traffic, lost cats – or as momentous as graduations, weddings, illness, death, divorce.

Individuals on any given day can be caught up in Life Happens! The key is how we respond – we make adjustments for the temporary detours each of us will sometime experience. Oprah Winfrey best exemplifies this, a person who had to play the hand she was dealt.

We hear her household name. We read about her life. We revel in her accomplishments. And the theme that resonates with us is her perseverance. Nothing held her back!

Oprah Gail Winfrey was born in Kosclusko, Mississippi, in 1954 to a teenage single mother – and with that birth came hardship. She lived her early years with her grandmother, Hattie Mae Lee. They were so poor that Winfrey often wore dresses made of potato sacks. When Oprah was six, she moved to inner city Milwaukee to live with her mother, where she was raped at age nine and became pregnant at 14 but lost her child in his infancy. She struggled with drugs, was rebellious, and suffered years of abuse. At 14, she returned to the South to live with her father in Nashville, Tennessee. He made education her priority.

Oprah persevered. As a teenager, she worked in a grocery store and in the newsroom of a local black radio station. She was an honor student and won an oratory contest that secured her a scholarship to Tennessee State University, where she earned a degree in speech and the performing arts. She went on to become a successful news anchor, and in 1986, *The Oprah Winfrey Show*, a Chicago-based daytime talk show, was born. Within months, it went from last to first place in the ratings, overtaking Donahue as the highest rated talk show in Chicago.

Since those early days of success, she has co-founded the women's cable television network Oxygen. She is president of Harpo Productions (Oprah spelled backwards). Winfrey has co-authored five books and publishes two magazines. Her newest creation is OWN: The Oprah Winfrey Network. Oprah is both actor and producer of such productions as *The Color Purple, The Wedding, Their Eyes Were Watching God,* and *Beloved.* She was nominated for an Academy Award for her role as Sophie in *The Color Purple.*

Her convictions and values have allowed her to persevere and lead others to succeed as well. Nelson Mandela has praised Winfrey for overcoming her own disadvantaged youth to become a benefactor for others ... investing in their futures and their successes.

Oprah shares that she has "learned to rely on the strength I inherited from all those who came before me – the grandmothers, sisters, aunts, and brothers, whose spirits were tested with unimaginable hardships and yet survived." Her tenacity, her courage, her determination have allowed her to "stand up, face resistance, and walk through it," dealing with what life dealt her.

Her talk show, magazine, and TV network have made her the wealthiest female entertainer in the world and the first black billionaire in history. However, it has been her intelligence, her curiosity, her humor, and her empathy for others that have allowed her to overcome life's hardships, and make her the most influential woman in America, perhaps the world.

And it just keeps getting better!

Procrastination:
The P to Avoid

How soon "not now" becomes "never."
-Martin Luther
German Priest and Scholar

Procrastination is a self-imposed barrier that many leaders and their work teams face. Once a well thought-out vision, initiative, or project is designed, it is imperative for the leader to "do whatever it takes" to move that plan forward.

The age-old adage definitely applies here: don't put off until tomorrow what you can do today. As leaders of action, deal with the green people, accept that life happens and don't allow procrastination to rob you of success.

The first step a procrastinator must take to eliminate this deterrent to success in achieving our goals is to determine the reason for the procrastination. Only when that occurs can we apply the right strategy to eradicate the postponement of our accomplishments and the stress it brings to our lives.

What is Your Reason for Procrastinating?

Do you not like to deal with unpleasant tasks – like disciplining a teenager or staff member or returning a call to a complaining customer? Do you have too much work on your plate and no way to prioritize it? Are you unclear in what you need to do? Is a fear of change or failure causing you to procrastinate?

Once you identify the explanation for your procrastinating, determine a strategy to eliminate it and stay loyal to that strategy. Some strategies you might consider include the following:

- Identify the time of day you do your best work and then focus on your priority work during that time – even if it is really early in the morning. Make that time sacred to you and your work. Anticipate and alleviate interruptions during this time. It is your time to accomplish!

- Don't leave work each day without identifying the five things you want (or must) accomplish by the end of the next day. This creates a sense of urgency for the work. Many we work with have found this strategy alone has allowed them to prioritize the expectations and achieve "chunks" of that work on a daily basis. What used to be an overwhelming expectation is now a sense of accomplishment and satisfaction.
- Set goals and determine achievable actions to accomplish the goals. Be SMART about your goals – make sure they are specific, measurable, attainable, results driven, and time bound. Visualize yourself in action! Replicate that vision in real life. Monitor the implementation of those actions on a daily or weekly basis. What gets monitored gets done!
- Organize your workspace so that your priority work is easily accessible. Use color-coded folders to prioritize the projects and their deadlines. Try a tickler file that is a daily reminder of what needs to be accomplished. Streamline your work and your life.
- Identify the energy drainers and gainers in your life. Eliminate those things that bog you down and capitalize on those things that energize you – yes, maybe even exercise.
- Try the 4 D's when work, including e-mails, comes your way:
  » First, ask yourself if this is something that really needs to be accomplished; if not, delete it from your list.
  » Then ask yourself if there is someone else who would do this job much better than you; if so, delegate it with clear expectations and support.
  » Third, ask yourself if this is something that must be accomplished today; if not, delay it with an expected completion date. Put it in your tickler file.

» Finally, if those three questions have been answered appropriately and the work is still in front of you, just do it and get it off your plate!

- Reward yourself. A job well done within the expected time frame deserves a well-earned treat – whether it's a trip to Europe or fifteen minutes of "me time" over a cup of coffee and a good book.

All of us procrastinate sometimes. However, don't make it a habit if you expect to persevere and accomplish your goals. And if you must procrastinate, choose to do it on those things that have little impact on your success. Revisit the Pareto principle we talked about in Human Being 101 – and put 80% of your effort on the top 20% of those tasks that get the results you want and need.

Taking action is a must! While you are developing the green people in your organization, dealing with life as it happens, and eliminating procrastination, you steadily move toward your goals. Let your team see your values in action when you are persevering through the difficult times. Be the Ulysses in their lives – the individual who commits to the long journey in achieving his goal, the individual who was willing to spend ten long years seeking his return home.

President Kennedy's Challenge

Setting Sail for the Moon

In a speech many decades ago, President John F. Kennedy presented a bold vision to a joint session of the United States Congress. He challenged our country "to commit itself to achieving the goal, before the decade is out, of landing a man on the Moon, and returning him safely to Earth." Kennedy truly believed the country possessed the resources and talents to achieve this goal, one that many could not initially conceive as possible.

The catalyst for the President's challenge was the

Soviets' success in beating the Americans at every milestone of space exploration. They had launched the Sputnik satellite into orbit and achieved the first man in space.

Although technically daunting, landing a man on the moon would vault the United States into first place in the race with the Soviets. Kennedy underscored the challenge: "No single space project in this period will be more impressive to mankind, or more important for the long-range exploration of space; and none will be so difficult or expensive to accomplish." President John F. Kennedy believed in the ingenuity and commitment of the people of our country; he then challenged us "to get it done!"

Thoughts become words.
Words become actions.
Actions become habits.
Habits become character
And character is everything.
-Author Unknown

Despite the skeptics who thought it was impossible, on July 20, 1969, a little more then eight years later, Neil Armstrong, the American Commander of Apollo 11 took a small step for man but a giant leap for mankind ... and completed the initial moon mission signifying America's leadership in space exploration.

Think about a time you wanted to give up, but realized you needed to keep on trying, to persist and achieve – to just do it. What were the barriers? What carried you through these roadblocks? Who helped you with the detours?

Perseverance:
Celebrating the Evidence of the Progress

Perseverance takes time! And if we don't take time to recognize and celebrate the progress we have made along the way, we rarely stay in "for the long haul."

*Show me how I am
making a difference
and I will keep
working.*

-Authors of
When Life Meets
Leadership

We must steward and model our vision, not just hang it on a wall, if people are going to stick with us. They need to see how the puzzle pieces of their work have come together, how their effort is making an impact. When you provide the evidence of progress – when you show them how they are making a difference, you give your team the gift of hope and the catalyst for change.

Give credit where credit is due. Provide your team with concrete examples of the obstacles they have overcome. Share the stories of how they tied a knot and hung on when they thought they were at the end of their rope. Share the small successes, noting how the links of those successes made the chain of accomplishments stronger. As the leader, learn to take responsibility when things go wrong.

And never underestimate the power your words or actions can have on the life of others as they persevere through the trials of their own lives. Marlo Thomas, in her book *The Right Words at the Right Time*, shares her own story and those of a hundred others when words made all the difference. Remember that no remarks you make will be trivial – someone will rely on your utterances to give them strength during the tough times; others will take on a "bet me" attitude if your words are discouraging. Make sure your words help make a life, not diminish it. Marlo Thomas adored her father, Danny Thomas, and spent many hours just observng him be successful – whether it be watching him shave early in the morning, cuing his lines for an upcoming movie, or working through St. Jude's to make life easier for a family hurting.

When it came time to prove her own skills in the business, she was often compared to her famous father. Can she act as well? Is she as funny? Will the legend live on through her? Discouraged, she shared her problem with her dad – her last name. He remarked, "I raised you to be a thoroughbred. When thoroughbreds run they wear blinders to keep their eyes focused straight ahead with no distractions, no other horses. They hear the crowd but they don't listen. They just run their own race." Thomas blazed her own trail, starring as television's first single woman living alone in a large city. She has produced multiple television specials, written books for children, and won awards for both her career and her humanitarian efforts for children with cancer.

Marlo Thomas has "run her own race." She is the National Outreach Director for St. Jude Children's Research Hospital and hosts A Place of Hope, documenting the lifesaving work of St. Jude.

What steps might you take to strengthen evidence of progress along the way – yours and those you influence? What words do you choose to assure they have a positive impact on others? How are you running your own race?

Bottom Line:
Remember the Turtle Won!

Remember Aesop's fable of the tortoise and the hare? Because the hare constantly taunted the tortoise for her slowness, the tortoise challenges the ridiculing hare to a race. The hare, of course, sprints off leaving the tortoise far behind. Confident of winning, this "rascally rabbit" takes a nap only to find his competitor crawling slowly but steadily across the finish line. The turtle chose something he wanted to stick with; he, unlike the rabbit, connected perseverance to his passion and won the race.

That is a lesson well learned and here are a few nuggets for your consideration as you persevere:

- People want to know that, regardless of the circumstances life gives us, you will be there for the journey.
- Purpose is greater than any individual task, project, or initiative. Ample time must be given in order for the greater purpose to be achieved.
- People need to see your passion – passion that doesn't wither away with time or difficult circumstances.
- Remember that in the confrontation between the stream and the rock, the stream always wins, not through strength, but through perseverance.
- And in life, there seems to be lots of us turtles!

The Challenge

Our challenge to each of you: Internalize the power of perseverance. Make it the mortar that cements the people, passion, and purpose of Your Framework. Remember that it is the dash that defines your life.

 Zen Wisdom:
In the end, floodwalls count upon every one of their bricks for success.

Reflection: Let's take a few minutes to reflect on the Power of Perseverance.

What?	So what?	Now what?
What have I learned about the power of perseverance?	And what are the implications for my life, my work, my family?	Now what are the steps I am going to take to assure my team and I persevere in making dreams come true?

CHAPTER 6
When Life Meets Leadership
Bottom Line

Live the Promise of People, Purpose, Passion,
and Perseverance

As the drafts of each of the preceding chapters of our book began to take shape, hours were spent reading, rereading, reflecting, and rewriting each. It soon became clear that this chapter should highlight the bottom line of the four P's using as a guide our original mantra – Simple, Compelling, and Balanced.

Two questions we asked ourselves:

- What exactly is it we hope readers of this book will take away?
- What impact can they count on in their lives and their leadership?

In answering these two questions, "a promise was born." Simply said, you can trust that People, Purpose, Passion, and Perseverance will make the difference in your life and leadership. Let's look now at how Practice and Personalization will allow you to live the Promise.

Practice:
Intersection at the Corner of Life and Leadership

Right now, at countless road intersections everywhere parades of people meet, briefly sharing their lives as drivers, passengers, and pedestrians. Most never even know for whom they waited. When the light changes, many continue on toward their destiny, perhaps never to meet again. We all join these dances daily without even thinking about them.

Occasionally, however, we stop just being travelers or pedestrians and actually allow ourselves to become present at the intersection. Our attention begins to connect with people around us and we start responding to them in personal ways. We wave back at the toddler gesturing at us from her car seat. We pull up to the stalled vehicle and offer our help to the young driver. We jump out of our car to push the senior citizen's cart over the curb.

When the right time and place converge, we cease being anonymous and our choices change the energy and directions of those sharing the intersection with us. When we choose to practice the four P's, we transform the lives we meet at the corners of Life and Leadership.

Join us in seeing how four individuals "tried on the four P's for size," internalizing each through conscious practice and reflection every day.

How Can I Help?

It is amazing how people react when you start with the positive and then offer help. This is a new approach that I have to intentionally think about before initiating conversations, but it is clear it effectively reaps positive results. Just yesterday during our school-wide Fun Day, I had to address the misbehavior of a challenging third grader, who made his feelings about me perfectly clear – and his adjectives were definitely not complimentary. I drew on my knowledge that my earlier interaction with him had not produced the desired results. So this time, I started with a positive and complimented his appropriate behavior earlier in the day. Then I moved to what was inappropriate and asked him, 'What can I do to help?' He thought for a moment and then responded, 'I really do know what I need to do,' and he adjusted his behavior for the rest of the day.

Now, I just need to practice, practice, practice! Through repetition I know I will transition from having to stop to think about what I will say to automatically leading with a positive and 'How can I help?'

-Sue R.

Using the Black Lab Method

No matter what, my black lab loves me uncondi-tionally. I can yell at him in the morning, but when I get home from work he greets me at the door, wagging his tail. When I encounter people who are difficult to work with, like the green people, I usually avoid them. Having recognized my mistake, I now apply the black lab method: I greet them lovingly every time I see them, no matter how I feel about our last encounter together. So far it is working. I am building better and more productive relationships with my co-workers.

-Jaclyn B.

I Will, No Matter What, I Will!

True to the era in which I was born, as a young woman I graduated from high school, married, and quickly bore two children. I often was left to raise them on my own because my husband was a travel-ling salesman. Becoming divorced when I was still in my 20's, I knew I needed to show my kids what they and I could become. While working full time at various odd jobs, I put myself through college and at age 32, I became a first-year teacher. At fifty, I am a proud mom of two young adults (really four, counting their spouses), the grandmother of two adorable grand-kids and looking forward to the third. It was a tough journey at times for all of us; well worth it, however, when I saw the tears in my dad's eyes as I crossed the stage to receive my doctorate in education.

-Susan P.

Making Our Private Label Swimwear

Two friends from different shores, Lake Panorama in Iowa and the Pacific Ocean, began our quest for the perfect swimsuit. We wanted it to fit here and there! After endlessly searching but finding nothing, the a-ha moment dawned, we would have to create our own. We made sure the suits fit our own curves! Sunbathers on both beaches admired the results, and coveted the design. M-m-m, perhaps a passion could become a partnership! Never intending to become entrepreneurs, Private Label Swimwear went into production.

-Mary and Betty

The Challenge

Our challenge to you: Give yourself permission to practice the four P's, and even to make mistakes with them. We learn from mistakes if we reflect on them.

Personalization:
Extending the Four P's

Once comfortable with the four P's, you will extend your Framework with additional P's that ignite your leadership and your life. Here are a few of those P's that people have shared with us.

Pacify

I recently had to come to the conclusion that I have spent most of my life pacifying people – not wanting to hurt their feelings, not wanting to make waves, not wanting to be seen.

Now I understand that making it better for others for the sake of peace often meant crushing my own spirit. It is only when I come out from behind myself and am honest and real that I can truly share and have an impact. I am finally able to embody the real me.

I no longer play the game of pacification; 'the

authentic me' is respected and valued by my friends and colleagues. Go natural!

-**Mary B.**

Painting

Throughout my life the road has been bumpy at times, but always rewarding and filled with a passel of learning. One of those important lessons was the need to help people see the big picture. Always before I had recognized pockets of excellence among our team but it wasn't until we started to paint the big picture that we became a real team – committed to achieving our vision.

Being a leader is not about them or me, but it is about community – all of us working together to achieve the big picture. Empowering others to learn all they can and be the best they can be brings focus to our vision.

-**Kyle P.**

Peace

Since the death of our infant son last Thanksgiving, I have searched for peace. It is the one thing in my life that eludes me most. There are days that my emotions bring me to my knees. Trystan's death has wounded me to the core. It has left me stripped of my faith, angry, jealous – you name an emotion and I have walked a day in its shoes.

I have a 45-minute commute each day to and from work. There are days when I arrive exhausted from thinking. Sometimes sitting and reflecting in the silence of your thoughts is a frightening and lonely place to be.

I do see the value of finding balance in my life, and maybe balance is a skill I have learned over the past few months. Even though I grieve, I am still a mother to a beautiful little girl, I am still a wife, I am still a daughter, and I am still a friend, a sister, a colleague, a teacher, a supervisor, and a leader. Being able to be these things to others while I feel I am pulling myself up by the bootstraps on a daily basis is the ultimate balancing act.

Late one afternoon my father and I began work on a memorial butterfly garden for Trystan. As I dug in the dirt, laid the forms for the cement and looked at the view from where the bench will be placed, I realized that by creating this garden I was giving our son a name and a place in this world – in my world. Even though he didn't get a chance to live in it here with us, we will be able to live in this place with him.

For the first time in a long time, I was comforted. Maybe peace is more than a state of mind. Maybe, for some of us, it is a place.

-Gretchen K

People vs. Paper

Why did I allow the paperwork of my job to overshadow the precious relationships I valued with my colleagues and family? It wasn't unusual for me as a young teacher to stay up until the wee hours of the morning assuring that all students' papers were corrected. As a principal, I did the same, giving up family time at the lake cabin to assure that all reports were ready for Monday morning. In addition, the house had to be spotlessly clean, all laundry done, meals prepared for the week, and countless errands accomplished. Oh, was I the E-Woman – doing everything but missing out on everybody!

Lessons have been learned and I am pleased now to assure that people trump the paper in my life!

-Ruth H.

Pillow Test

We live in a very fast-paced society, and it is often hard to find time to really stop to think about anything. Instead of intentionally reflecting on something I have done or said, I just end up breezing past and moving on to the next thing because I don't have time. This 'no time' mentality makes my free moments even more valuable. That is why I must find ways to utilize those minutes for thought and reflection. This is a new discovery for me and I truly believe it is an integral part of effective leadership and being a good person. One of the times I have found that is available for thought and reflection is when I lay down at night. Before I fall asleep, I am able to replay the events of the day, the things I have accomplished, and how I am feeling.

When I put my head on the pillow, it is, in many cases, the moment of truth. It's when I am able to really analyze what's going on, whether it be challenges or celebrations. And more importantly, not just what's going on, but how I am responding to those situations.

The pillow test has allowed me to plan to respond effectively, not just react.

-Nicole T

Patterns

I have been a person who judges people instantly. This is a pattern in my life that I need to eliminate. I know now I need to work on building a relationship with them as I continue to form a more honest opinion of these people. I will work on this and keep my mouth shut until I get to really know them. Responding vs Reacting – this is the key! My mother reminds me of this almost daily as I am quick to react. I think the strategy to making this happen is listening! If you take a breath, think, and listen, then you can respond without making a snap judgment about people.

-Rachel R.

Priorities

I think everyone one of us can relate to my mother's adage, 'Be sure you have on clean underwear and socks!'

Deep down, I knew she was right. Taking care of me must be the first priority. I simply cannot be effective in anything I do if I don't!

Of course, this required a brutally honest conversation with myself. I had to answer the question, 'What's the best use of my time and energy?' I also had to realize there would be times I couldn't do it all myself. I was reminded again of my mother and her wisdom, 'Sometimes you can't and you just need to ask for help.

In today's complex world, I keep my priorities straight and encourage those who work with me to do the same. As a result, we are all now more likely to trust each other, pitch in, and get the work done.

Get your priorities straight – and your underwear clean!
-Kiersten H.

The Challenge

Our challenge to you: Extend your own framework! Identify those P's that need attention in your life and will actually help strengthen the original four P's of your framework. P's are pathways and connections to others and yourself. Maybe what you find for yourself doesn't even start with P – that's OK, the key is to have your own memory peg to use as a reminder.

Living the Promise!

The intersection of life and leadership happens on many scales. Sometimes it is the interaction of only two individuals; sometimes it involves a cast of hundreds. It always starts with people, is sparked by concern, and is remarkably fueled by care. The four P's live every day around us.

Sam's Story

An Intersection of Choice

Sam was a fifth grader with a tough reputation, a challenging home life, and an attitude that never produced a smile. Bill, a school administrator, recognized him as "a kid who definitely was struggling but who also carried someone better inside." Years passed and occasionally Bill saw Sam in the halls of the school. One day the guidance counselor said to Bill, "You know Sam, don't you? Would you have a talk with him?"

Sam was about to start his senior year in high school and yet the day before he had been sentenced to thirty days in jail. He spent a hard night in his cell, crying himself to sleep. The next day brought a surprise visitor. At first he was confused when he spied Bill in the doorway. "What does he want with me?" Sam broke down when Bill managed to have him released from jail on the promise that he would not be back. Sam began his senior year on time with his classmates but was required to check in with Bill each day. At first he felt like he was in trouble or being treated like a convict.

Bill recalled, however, more details about those first meetings. Sam still was not smiling and his tough demeanor had reappeared. When Bill remarked, "What's this I hear about you not coming to school sometimes?" The next moment was a powerful one for Sam, as he fought to exclaim through his tears, "You wouldn't come to school either if you smelled like shit!" Bill learned that Sam had been kicked out of his home and was living in an unheated garage with an old couch and hot plate. Sam was making ends meet by working in a hog confinement facility – hence, the aforementioned smell.

Bill sprang into action. Within minutes at Bill's home, they found groceries in the pantry, selected a couple of pairs of jeans, and managed to find enough socks, underwear, and college sweatshirts that would outfit this high school senior. Calls to the community produced a place for Sam to live. Plans were made to assure clean clothes as Sam dropped off at Bill's office his dirty clothes each morning and picked up clean clothes before heading out to the bus at night.

Things seemed to be going along really well. Bill remembers that Sam was coming to school regularly, doing well in his classes, and even found a girl he was interested in. One day, Bill received a call that Sam was again in the county jail – this time for having broken a restraining order established by the girlfriend's parents, who did not approve of Sam. Bill remembers, "Sam was as broken as I had ever seen anyone. I asked Sam to trust me once more ... and we together would work it out."

Bill invited Sam to help him with chores at his home on the weekend. "The kid was amazing, a hard worker, and wonderful at everything mechanical." Bill recalled enthusiastically, "We always mixed fun with work and always, always had lots of conversations." The two covered everything – hopes, dreams, and challenges. Sam once asked, "Do you think I can do this someday, have a place like this?" Bill responded without hesitation, "Absolutely. Make it your goal. And everything has to be pointed toward this purpose."

After Sam's graduation from high school, he enlisted in the United States Army and chose what the recruiter said was the hardest career, Airborne Infantry. Sam wanted to challenge himself beyond his known limits. As an expert mortar man, Sam earned the rank of E5 Sgt, receiving numerous commendations. He served tours in Iraq and Afghanistan and was honorably discharged. All through his service, he kept in contact with Bill.

Upon returning to the states from his last tour, Sam decided to make Fairbanks, Alaska, his home. Sam's life continued a pattern of positive choices. Today he lives in a lovely home with his wife, Darrah, and their beautiful daughter, Haylea, and works as a Boiler Feed Water Technician at the Fort Wainwright Army base.

Sam often reflects on his story, "I feel I have cheated death many times in combat. I live each day as if it were my last. That night when I was in jail changed my life. I will never forget the hand that reached out to me. Bill inspired me not to have fears, to reach for the stars, and to smile every chance I have."

The Miners' Story

An Intersection by Chance

Mining for minerals deep below the earth's surface is dangerous and uncertain work. It's unforgiving! People toil for a living by risking their lives below for the success of those above. Accidents happen and often become tragedies when the circumstances turn deadly for those trapped by their livelihood.

On August 5, 2010, the earth crumbled inside a remote gold and copper mine in northern Chile; 33 miners became trapped a half mile underground in what was to become the longest confinement in history. It was a miracle they were all alive! And it would take another miracle, many days and nights and hundreds of hands, to bring them to the sunlight.

For the first 17 days after the cave-in, not knowing if or when they would be found, the miners calmly rationed every other day two bites of tuna fish, half a cookie, and a half cup of milk per person. The first sign of life from the miners for those gathered above came on August 22nd when knocking was heard on a drill head. As the drill surfaced it held a note, "The 33 of us in the shelter are well." That shelter would become the miners' home for 69 days, and they quickly realized they would have to support one another to survive. They were as individual as the requests they sent to the surface. One wanted Elvis music piped in, one proposed to his partner of 25 years, and a third celebrated his 34th birthday underground. Genuinely building relationships, capitalizing on the strengths of each, and recognizing every contribution, the men built their own community.

The trapped men had one purpose – stay alive to get out! The rescuers and families had one purpose – bring them home alive! Survival was the heartbeat of both groups, and it was the ultimate worthwhile work – preserving human life. To that end both groups would explore every possibility. Experts from around the world lent their medical, nutritional, and engineering skills. Food, supplies, and medicine were sent down the small shaft to keep the men healthy. The miners were advised to stay on a 48-hour cycle despite the darkness and to complete exercise routines. Up top the rescuers had their own challenges, scorching heat during the day and bone-chilling cold at night.

A professor of psychiatry, Dr. Jon Shaw, expressed that people who endure a harrowing experience tend to take a hard look at their lives and what gives them purpose and meaning. Passions beyond survival rode high with each miner and those passions, often similar, were expressed with deep conviction. Jimmy Lagues wrote this touching note to his wife; "There are actually 34 of us because God has never left us down here." Forty-year-old Mario Espinace described his dilemma, "I think I had extraordinary luck. I was with God and with the devil. And I reached out for God." Up top, Priscilla Avalos said it this way, "We have prayed to San Lorenzo, the patron saint of miners, and to many other saints so that my brothers Florencio and Renan would come out of the mine all right ... ." And on a lighter note, Franklin Lobos, who played for the Chilean National Soccer Team, came out of the mine sharing the excitement of his passion by bouncing a ball on his foot and knee.

If any crisis exemplifies perseverance it would be this one. Above and below ground everyone had to cultivate a sense that together we can do this. Then they had to do it! From the first time the bucket-like Phoenix lowered into the mine, and miner #1 stepped aboard the capsule to rise up the 2,041-foot escape shaft, no one doubted the day-to-day struggle had taken a supreme effort and endurance. The crowd in Camp Hope threw confetti, released balloons, and sprayed champagne as the last man, the coal miners' leader Luis Urzua, surfaced. Chile's president, the rescue workers, and their foreman all joined in a rousing rendition of their national anthem. The miracle was complete!

Truly this will gain legendary status as a story of hope, international cooperation, and a testament to the human spirit. These 33 miners and their rescuers achieved their purpose, all alive and on the surface, through their own passion and perseverance!

Stop, Look, Listen, and Engage to Achieve the Promise!

Our actions, whether one to one like Bill and Sam or with hundreds working together to save the Chilean miners, can impact our own lives and the lives of others if we are willing to become engaged. When we stop, look, and listen – whether on a busy city street, a high mountain road, the hallways of a school, or the shaft of a mine – we begin to live the very intersections of life and leadership that form the basis of this book.

Reflection: Teacher's Opinion

Learning a lot about yourself

My perspective on leadership as a classroom teacher who taught government and civics was that at any given time each one of us will be placed in a position of leadership whether we want it or not, it is just going to happen to you. How you respond to the challenge, whether you chose it or it chooses you will tell a lot about yourself and give you that chance to adjust your values, your perspective and your goals.

-Terry K.

Leadership helps recognize needs, directions, opportunities, and sustainability. It is necessary because life's journey is not about its endpoints but the substantial space and time in between them. Note that we spend most of our time in the dash – that critical convergence of actions, relationships, meaning, energy, and commitments that fill and sustain our markers for progress. We will start. We will stop. But most importantly, we will connect the dash with many mini-dashes. These provide the opportunities for us to refine our work in order to achieve our goals together.

Refinement, too, comes through mistakes and learning. A successful journey may start from a single straight line, out of the harbor to open sea, but the destination is only won by many course corrections in response to weather and tides. Mistakes need not be endpoints of our dash. They are an opportunity to pause and examine our assumptions and perspectives. They can actually be trials and valuable discoveries in clever disguise. Diversity in viewpoints and abilities can always help address important steps to take next. Steve Jobs, one of the founders of Apple Computer, told students at their Stanford University graduation in 2005 that when he was fired from Apple by the person he had hired to help lead it, he struggled at first to understand his mistakes. It was a painful time, yet he came to understand that it allowed him to examine his passions and perspectives. He realized he loved what he was doing. He restarted himself with NeXT Computer and PIXAR. He learned and allowed himself to grow into his dash – he was not at an endpoint at all.

This brings back to us, too, the importance of front-door and backdoor leadership. Both roles contribute to the effectiveness of an individual and a team. People rise to the occasion when their abilities can mean the most. Recognizing these potentials in others, whether from a front-door authority like Bill with Sam or a backdoor member of the team, like the rescuers of the Chilean miners, is essential as leadership intersects with life. Above all, we must create and support spaces for both styles to flourish in their dynamic journeys forward. Leadership is inclusive, not exclusive. When we lead, we do so as we live – not alone or apart from others. We move together and everyone contributes. All members lead in their own time, offering their passion to the mix. The results mean shared credit for the final result.

Both Sam's story and the story of the Chilean miners underscore an important lesson for us. Simply put, trust is a gift. Trust is a pattern of behavior over time, and we must give the gift to ourselves before we can share it with others. Our framework is bound by trust. We express value in others by having faith in them on the shared path.

Ultimately, the promise of The Framework lives through you. People with Purpose applying Passion to achieve Perseverance will reach their Potential. Opportunity meets Action at the corners of Life and Leadership. Practice makes permanent, too. The words on these pages can only become reality if they are practiced and guide your life. If unused or forgotten, the benefits of each idea diminish the impact of The Framework. Remember, though, you are not alone. One person can be the spark at the right moment, but it is ultimately the group that must carry its parts into the shared future. Sharing the load makes for lighter work.

Reflection also provides insight. It challenges your thinking and your work. It fosters creative interactions and continuous improvements. For the group, it provides stories that reinforce evidence of accomplishment. Reflection is key for living well and making the dash work to your benefit. The results mean that better becomes the best in the end.

The Challenge

Our challenge to you: Prepare and Promote! Gain first a clear understanding of The Framework and its ties to your leadership and life. Then encourage others' awareness of The Framework, always fostering practice of the four P's by your team.

 Zen Wisdom:
No matter where you start, life and leadership always begin with we.

About the authors

Bill Wright

A *former superintendent of schools and now a consultant to businesses on leadership, explains* **People** *incentives, interactions and relationships.*

Elaine Smith-Bright

A *former teacher, school administrator and currently a clinical professor of leadership at a university, elevates everyday actions to a higher plateau of* **Purpose** *and meaning.*

Lou Howell

An *author of three education books and a director of a nonprofit organization, represents* **Perseverance**, *recognizing that working against the odds can produce large rewards.*

John Fujii

A *leader in the technical and educational world of computer graphics and animation, exemplifies* **Passion** *for one's professional activities.*